OUR URBAN FUTURE

THE
Crystal
A Sustainable Cities Initiative
by Siemens

BOOKLINK

Los Angeles skyline

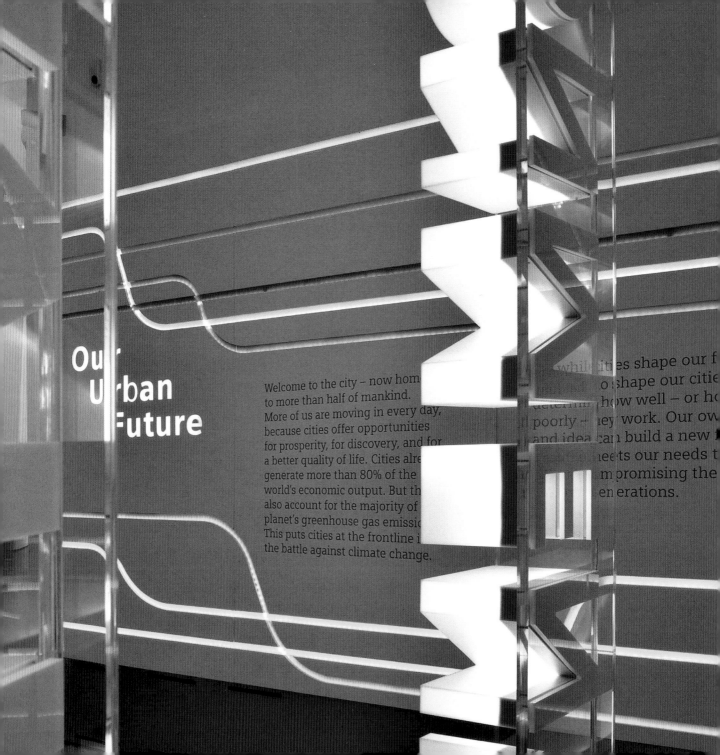

Our Urban Future

Welcome to the city – now home to more than half of mankind. More of us are moving in every day, because cities offer opportunities for prosperity, for discovery, and for a better quality of life. Cities already generate more than 80% of the world's economic output. But they also account for the majority of planet's greenhouse gas emissions. This puts cities at the frontline in the battle against climate change.

...while cities shape our f... ...to shape our cities... ...how well – or how ...poorly – they work. Our own ...and ideas can build a new ...meets our needs t... ...compromising the ...generations.

It is showing what urban life is going to be like and the way in which we can all work together to improve our cities.

Boris Johnson, Mayor of London, speaking about The Crystal, 2012.

Introduction

The Crystal has been designed as a place to start a conversation about sustainable cities. In planning the exhibition, Siemens wanted to avoid sustainability and futurology clichés. You won't find any Blade Runner-style images of a bleak dystopia here. Nor will displays nag you. Instead the exhibition shows that, while sustainability is a challenge, the solutions to achieving it are well within our grasp.

Smart, smart, smart. You'll notice the word everywhere at the Crystal. That's because 'smart' is the key to sustainable cities: thinking holistically, thinking ahead, drawing on the best technologies and analysis. Those principles have also been applied to the design of the exhibition.

Real and sensational

'Real and sensational' was Siemens' brief for the exhibition design.

Walking the talk

Throughout the design process, the creative team wanted to prove that it 'walked the talk'. It wasn't enough to talk about sustainability – sustainability had to be embedded in the design.

Throughout the exhibition you'll see examples of what a sustainable building looks like: use of sustainable material, black water being recycled, rainwater harvested, ground source and solar energy collection, and everywhere, smart technology ensuring that the building runs efficiently and well. The Crystal shows us that sustainability doesn't have to be harder or uglier or more expensive, but can be used to create better cities and, ultimately, better lives for their inhabitants.

When designing the exhibition, I always imagined the eight-year-old me – what would fascinate me? Real electric, real water, real living plants … things to touch and stuff that would make me ask 'how did they do this?'

Dan Savage, Exhibition Designer,
Event Communications.

Live lab

The story-led exhibition has been designed as a 'live lab' where you can get hands-on with the problems and have fun engaging with some of the technologies that point to the way forward. Play is the most fundamental way of learning and everyone – from school children to city managers – is encouraged to have a go and enjoy engaging with the exhibits.

Mega, Macro, Micro

The exhibition is divided into three areas: Mega, Macro and Micro. The Mega area looks at three global megatrends that are changing our world: demographic change, urbanization and climate change. The Macro zones present solutions on a city level: how should we plan our cities now and in the future? The Micro elements are woven throughout the exhibition but come together in the final Future Life experience. They look at how individuals can affect sustainability – and what urban life might look like as a result.

Individual zones are all broadly based around a common structure. Each one has an 'attractor' display that sums up the

Our
Urban
Future

Welcome to the city – now home
to more than half of mankind.
More of us are moving in every day
because cities offer opportunities
for prosperity, for discovery, and for
a better quality of life. Cities already
generate more than 80% of the
world's economic output. But they
also account for the majority of our
planet's greenhouse gas emissions.
This puts cities at the frontline in
the battle against climate change.

Enviro...

Sustainable cities st...

theme, along with a series of displays that present the challenges, the solutions – and the results of any activities you may have taken part in. While there is a common structure at the core, each display area has its own distinct personality, color palette and suite of activities.

Where to start?

The exhibition has a fixed start and end point. In between, you're invited to explore wherever and however you like. Everything in the exhibition is connected (just as everything in our cities is connected) so it will make sense, no matter in what order you experience the displays.

The exhibition opens with the Introduction. Here you'll find one of

The Crystal building is the first in the world to achieve both BREEAM (BRE Environmental Assessment Method) 'outstanding' and LEED (Leadership in Energy and Environmental Design) 'platinum' ratings.

Colin Cassé, Head of Projects, Siemens.

the most important questions: what are sustainable cities? Three vertical, illuminated typographic displays represent three things that need to be in balance – supported by good governance - to achieve sustainable cities: Quality of Life, Economics and Environment. These elements feed into the content of all displays.

Running from the Introduction are colored threads, each one representing

a different display zone. Follow the exhibition upstairs to the Mezzanine and the start of your journey in Forces of Change.

The Crystal key

The Crystal key tag issued at reception enables you to 'log in' to displays and have your activities and areas of interest saved. You will then be able to access a record of your experiments in the Future Life zone.

Cities are the economic powerhouses of the future and also the place where most of the CO$_2$ emissions occur in the world. The answers to a sustainable approach in cities require a balanced view between economics, quality of life of their citizens and a strong environmental care. Low carbon cities are the ones which will prosper, attract more people, foster new businesses and become resilient forces on their own.

Pedro Pires de Miranda, Corporate Vice President, Siemens AG.

WHY CITIES?

Introduction

Cities take up less than two percent of the world's landmass. Despite their small geographic coverage they have a huge impact on the world and how we live. They are centers for the economy, for communication and for culture. Cities can drive new ideas and beliefs. Cities can innovate and they are constantly evolving and changing. But cities can also have negative impacts on the local environment – the air we breathe and the water we drink. They can also provide the conditions for social issues such as isolation and crime. Cities can often have extremes of wealth and poverty within their geographic boundaries.

Cities in ancient times

Many of the drivers behind the growth of cities and the motives for the migration of populations to cities remain unchanged throughout human history. Between 4000 and 3200 BC the city of Uruk, which is regarded as one of the first cities led the urbanisation of Sumer, an ancient civilization in southern Mesopotamia (which now lies in modern Iraq). At its height in 2900 BC as many as 80,000 people had abandoned their villages and flocked to Uruk. During this period of history, city states began to dominate Mesopotamia. As their rulers and citizens became more influential they demanded more goods either through conquest or trade. The city also required skills and trades as it grew. For example the building of the city wall, ordered by King Gilgamesh required expertise in design and construction.

New York City

Mesopotomia was the location for many important cities in the ancient world.

During this period many cities were built and destroyed in Mesopotamia between the fertile plains of the Euphrates and the Tigris. Possibly the most famous was Babylon – founded in 1894 BC. Babylon twice expanded to become an important world empire before it was finally absorbed by Persia. It grew to become an important place for administration, culture and learning. Yet its beginnings were provided for by its fertile plains irrigated by dykes from the River Euphrates. This environment provided bountiful harvests of fruit, vegetables and grain. Coupled with supporting herds of sheep and cattle, the Babylonians were able to trade surplus crops and livestock for raw materials such as timber, gold and copper. These materials were then crafted into goods – weapons, furniture, jewellery, which could then be traded. Babylon's location meant that as well as its natural resources it could trade easily with other areas. The lack of natural protection in Mesopotamia, eventually led to the fall of Babylon.

Babylon, one of the most famous early cities.

These examples from the ancient world illustrate some of the reasons why cities grow and thrive. They are important centres of trade, administration, justice, learning and culture. Their location is often close to natural resources or in locations of strategic importance for trade both regionally and globally – such as coastlines or next to rivers.

What makes a successful city?
Cities in the modern world continue to attract people to live and work. They are the powerhouses of the world economy. As communication gets easier and global markets become more accessible, the importance of cities continues to grow. Economic growth and urbanization have always been closely linked. No country has developed without the urbanization of its population. 60 percent of the world's Gross Domestic Product (GDP) is accounted for by just 600 urban areas. This trend will only become stronger, as the global population continues to grow and more and more people choose to move to cities. Around half of the world population lives in cities at the moment. The total population of our urban areas will reach 6.3 billion by 2050.

Johannesburg

We must plan for our cities of the future, to ensure that they continue to thrive. But we must also plan how we cope with some of the challenges created by cities. Cities consume huge amounts of resources such as water, electricity and food. They need large amounts of infrastructure to support transportation, communication, power and the use of other resources in our homes and workplaces. The consumption of resources and provision of infrastructure has impacts on both the local and global environment. For example cities produce vast quantities of waste that must be managed. They can also suffer from air pollution from their industries, homes and from transport.

Lisbon

Ultimately, successful cities are not simply those that generate economic activity. Whilst supporting economic activity, they must be sustainable and provide a good quality of life for their citizens. Global challenges such as climate change will ultimately be won or lost in cities, so we must find ways in which to make our cities more efficient, cleaner, resilient and great places to live in. This is crucial for supporting future generations and protecting the Earth's ecosystems.

Stockholm

So what makes a successful city? It is worth thinking for a moment about natural ecosystems. Natural ecosystems, such as rainforests have inbuilt systems and feedback loops to ensure that resources are used efficiently and that as little is wasted as possible. However, the modern city has a metabolism that is almost entirely a one-way process. The impact of cities is far reaching. Cities can import vast amounts of materials to sustain them that have impacts far beyond their boundaries and produce large quantities of waste products and residues to the environment. Cities consume 75 percent of energy and produce 80 percent of global emissions of greenhouse gases. Understanding how cities function and identifying ways in which we can improve aspects of it, such as how we use water, energy and how we manage our waste are essential to ensuring we create sustainable, livable cities which have lower impacts on the natural environment. In other words to create cities that mimic natural ecosystems, that are efficient and not wasteful.

Jakarta

Economic growth, sustainability and quality of life are three pillars that will support successful cities of the future. Cities that provide a good quality of life will be more attractive places to do business and to live. Cities that are sustainable and minimize their impact on the environment will provide high quality infrastructure and operate more efficiently. Future cities will need to be sustainable and provide a high quality of life in order to compete and thrive.

Cities are where change is happening the fastest and we must seize the opportunities we have been presented with to make that change significant and permanent.

David Miller, former Mayor of Toronto.

Improving city infrastructure, developing and implementing new technologies and changing the way people and businesses think and operate all form part of making our cities more competitive, prosperous, sustainable and great places to live. Cities need clean air, clean water and need to be safe and secure. They need efficient buildings, reliable energy grids and a range of transport solutions. These need to be brought together in a coherent and integrated way.

Rio de Janeiro

This book sets out some of the challenges facing cities in the 21st century. But it also shows the ways in which cities are taking on these issues and some of the technology that is available to address them. Cities have met challenges before, they are inspiring and they are innovative. The book concludes by examining what cities of the future could look like.

Melbourne has been named the world's most liveable city for the third year in a row.

Algiers

The heartbeat you hear inside the theatre belongs to my son, Leo. I recorded it during one of my wife's antenatal check ups.

Dan Savage, Exhibition Designer, Event Communications.

The mezzanine creates more space to tell the story of sustainable cities and it also provides an elevated platform for exploring global megatrends, while offering visitors an overview of the whole exhibition. From the mezzanine you have a view of all the macro zones and, within them, the challenges and the solutions inherent in developing sustainable cities. As well as providing a great view, the mezzanine tackles two important tasks – inspiring and informing audiences about the megatrends that are affecting the way we live now and in the future.

A glowing egg like structure balances on the edge of the mezzanine floor. Inside you find yourself in a fully immersive image and sound environment that appears to hang in space, with images floating on the walls and floor. The content is carefully designed to focus your attention on the megatrends. The three interlinking projected sequences paint a picture of demographic change, urbanization and climate change, the biggest issues affecting our daily life. The films blend still images, film clips, graphics,

sound and lighting to create an immersive experience that balances drama and statistics. The idea is to inspire people, to give a sense of the problems we face, but not send a message of doom and gloom. The future will be different – but it can still be beautiful.

Urbanization begins with the migration of animals, then humans, gradually showing the impact of migration on cities with a rain of passport stamps falling down the screen, representing today's multi-cultural metropolis. A giant wave sweeps viewers into a story of big weather events and climate change. Demographic change is introduced with a cascade of ultrasound images.

Out on the mezzanine floor, three displays provide more information on the three megatrends. The design of the Demographic change display is top-heavy, reflecting the top-heavy make-up of cities due to ageing populations. The lower level handrails enable visitors to focus on any of the rolling statistics and come 'face to face' with the people behind the numbers.

The urbanization exhibit was inspired by high-rise housing. Two towers form structures for interactivity, while real images of city dwellers are spliced together in a stylised collage skyscraper. Content examines different city types: emerging, transitioning, mature.

Climate change is represented by a stylised globe, divided into three sections. Before entering the Forces of Change theatre, visitors view the Earth as a whole; but when you leave you see that it's actually a fragmented structure. The design references the idea of alternative futures. You can engage with different models illustrating how climate change might affect the Earth.

Around the edge of the mezzanine are markers that point out the Macro zones on the floor below. The presence of the markers on the mezzanine is important, because they remind us that cities don't exist in a bubble. Every day city-dwellers and city planners are affected by the three megatrends.

Looking back, I underestimated the risks. The planet and the atmosphere seem to be absorbing less carbon than we expected, and emissions are rising pretty strongly. Some of the effects are coming through more quickly than we thought then.

Sir Nicholas Stern, World Economic Forum, January 2013, Davos.

Forces of Change

We are facing changes to the way we live. It is not sustainable to continue being so wasteful with the world's resources. It is said that if everyone in the world lived like the average North American, five Earths would be needed to sustain life. If everyone lived like the average European, we would need three Earths.

If everyone on Earth lived like the average North American, five planets would be needed to sustain life.

This example not only illustrates how wasteful we can be, it also shows a lack of equity in the world's resources and standards of living. Clearly we need to find ways in which the world's higher standards of living can be maintained but also enjoyed by all, without destroying the world we live in. Three significant issues face the planet. It is within the context of these megatrends that we must find a way to live sustainably.

Climate Change

The UK government asked Sir Nicholas Stern to lead a review on the economics of climate change which was published in 2007. It identifies climate change as the greatest and widest-ranging market failure the world has seen. It argued that the benefits of decisive and early action outweigh the costs of doing nothing. Just six years after publishing his report, the author now argues that he underestimated the risks from climate change.

Climate change is a megatrend facing the planet.

Global emissions of greenhouse gases are rising quickly. This year for the first time in human history CO_2 levels in our atmosphere rose above 400 parts per million (ppm). Governments agreed in 2010 at the UN Framework Convention on climate change in Mexico that the average global temperature increase must be checked at 2°C compared with pre-industrial age temperatures. Countries have agreed that a new global agreement on climate change must be reached by 2020.

There is broad agreement amongst the scientific community that stabilizing atmospheric concentrations of CO_2 at 450ppm, would result in a 50 percent chance of halting the now inevitable rise in global temperatures at 2°C. Yet globally we persist on stacking the odds against ourselves even higher.

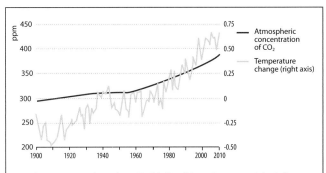

Note: The temperature refers to the NASA Global Land-Ocean Temperature Index in degrees Celsius, base period: 1951-1980. The resulting temperature change is lower than the one compared with pre-industrial levels.

Sources: Temperature data are from NASA (2013); CO_2 concentration data from NOAA Earth System Research Laboratory.

Source: IEA

World Atmospheric concentration of CO_2 and average global temperatures.

Atmospheric concentration of CO_2 has seen exponential growth since the 1960s. Worryingly some recent analysis suggests that impacts that had been assumed to occur with greater changes in temperature are in fact likely to happen with smaller increases in global temperatures. The risks thought to occur with a temperature rise of 2°C are now thought to happen with a rise of 1°C. Equally the risks that were previously considered to occur with an increase in global temperature of 4°C are more likely to occur with a temperature rise of 2°C.

Cities need to improve their resilience to weather events like flooding.

So what are the changes that we can expect? We can already see evidence of some of them. Sea levels have risen by 15-20 cm over the past century and have increased most rapidly in the last decade. The number of extreme weather events is increasing. The number and intensity of heat waves has increased, resulting in more droughts and harming food production. New York was hit by Hurricane Sandy in September 2011; its impact was catastrophic causing 286 deaths and costing the economy up to $50 billion. The Intergovernmental Panel on Climate Change (IPCC) state that it is virtually certain that substantial warming in temperature extremes will occur by the end of the 21st century; It is likely that both the frequency and proportion of precipitation that is heavy rainfall will increase globally and whilst the frequency of tropical cyclones is likely to remain the same, their wind speeds are likely to increase; It is very likely that sea levels will rise contributing to upward trends of extreme coastal high water.

The number of extreme weather events is increasing.

Cities need to be at the forefront of tackling climate change. C40 Cities Climate Leadership Group estimates that cities consume over two thirds of the world's energy and account for 70 percent of global greenhouse gas emissions. In addition almost 75 percent of urban settlements are located in coastal areas at risk of sea-level rise.

75 percent of urban settlements are located in areas at risk from sea-level rise.

Urbanization

Around half of the world's population now live in cities and urban areas compared with 30 percent in 1950. By 2050 this proportion is forecast to rise to 68 percent – that's 6.3 billion people, an increase of 2.7 billion in just under 40 years. The growth in urbanization is enough to absorb the entire increase in global population which is expected to rise by 2.3 billion over that period.

Shanghai, along with many other cities face rapid growth as more of the world's population live in cities.

The attraction of cities and urban areas is not a new phenomenon. For millennia people have been drawn towards the economic, cultural and social benefits and opportunities of living in large groups. Ancient Rome, the fastest growing city of its time attracted people from the countryside with the offer of work, clean water, entertainment, protection and food, often subsidized or free through the Annona or 'grain dole'.

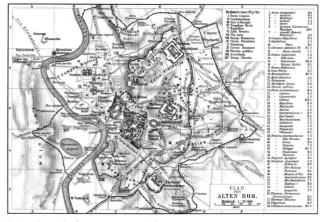

Ancient Rome, the fastest growing city of its time.

Living in cities can bring efficiencies in the use of resources. Travel distances to services and entertainment are less. The population density allows the development and greater use of public transport. London's CO_2 emissions per head of 5.9 tonnes are one tonne lower than the rest of the UK.

London produces less CO_2 per head than other regions of the United Kingdom.

But urbanization also brings with it challenges and adverse impacts which need to be managed. These can include congestion, air pollution, overcrowding, crime, pollution of waterways, loss of habitat, isolation and extremes of wealth and poverty. Over one billion people are living in urban slums which are often overcrowded, without clean water or basic services and polluted. Poverty is at present growing faster in urban areas than rural ones. Much of the continued urbanization will happen in regions of the world with less capacity to cope with the change.

City governments have to contend with the complexities of building and sustaining infrastructure, whilst meeting the needs of these huge and often growing populations. Those governing cities must balance competitiveness, quality of life and the environment in their decision making in order to maintain cities and make them vibrant, enjoyable and successful places to live and work.

Cities like Hong Kong have to balance economic competitiveness, quality of life and the environment to make them attractive places to live.

Demographic change
The world's population is forecast to grow from seven billion to nine billion in 2050 and ten billion by 2100. That growth is not evenly spread. Between 2011 to 2100 the population in developed countries will remain largely unchanged, growing from 1.24 billion to 1.34 billion (this relatively small growth will be driven by net migration from developing countries). Nearly all of the additional three billion people will live in developing countries.

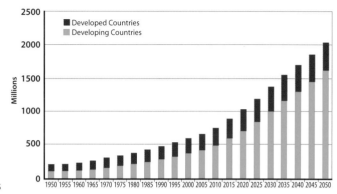

Number of people aged 60 or over: World, developed and developing countries, 1950–2050.

What are the implications of a larger older population? It will result in a shrinking workforce and will also impact the costs of social and health care. A study looking at the ageing population in the United States found that the number of people over 65 will increase by 135 percent between 2000 and 2050, and over 85 by 350 percent. The estimated proportion of GDP spent on health care and social security will rise from 6.8 percent to 13.2 percent accordingly.

Rising to the challenge
The world faces some serious challenges if we are to accommodate the changes in global population and demography and tackle the rising levels of CO_2 in our atmosphere. However, solutions do exist to help take these on. The following chapters look at issues facing cities and some of the options available to them.

Sea Levels have risen by 15-20cm over the past century and most rapidly in the last decade.

The interface is based on the Green City Index (GCI), sponsored by Siemens and conducted by The Economist Intelligence Unit. The index measures and ranks the environmental performance of leading cities worldwide, as well as their commitment to reducing their environmental impact.

Stefan Denig, Head of Communications & Marketing, Siemens Centre of Competence Cities.

Although you can experience the exhibition in any order, there is one Macro zone that connects to all the others: Creating Cities, identifiable by the city plan printed on the floor. After leaving Forces of Change, all visitors 'land' in the Creating Cities zone. Central to the design concept for the Crystal is the idea that you have to understand the mechanics and workings of a city as a total entity before looking at the individual elements which create it.

What does a well-designed city look like? This fundamental question is posed by the City Icon, a digital sculpture that can be seen from almost everywhere in the exhibition as well as from outside the Crystal. The City Icon is a complex system of interrelated parts, each part representing one of the Macro zones. Different parts are represented by different colours of LEDs and these create sequences of images. The Icon can look like a street map, or a medical diagnostic image, or an electricity network … The Icon communicates the idea that city decision makers need to be able to see all the 'parts' that make up a city to understand how they can work together. It acts as a beacon or centre of gravity for the whole exhibition.

The Icon also reminds us that everything in the city is related and that better cities are achieved by facilitating connectivity. An interface at the base of the City Icon enables you to explore the world's greenest cities. You might be surprised to see who's at the top of the list – and who's at the bottom.

The cityscape printed on the floor (which extends through to Keep Moving) provides a context for the displays, whose design language is inspired by graph paper and building blocks. Solutions appear to grow from the building blocks of sustainable technologies.

Understanding Cities is a bespoke interactive based on the data actually used by city managers at New York's Regional Planning Authority (RPA). It uses real time information and snapshot monitoring to paint a picture of how cities work. You can select from a number of key areas to focus on.

City Shapes is a matrix of LEDS set into wireframe interactive 3D city that illustrates land use in relation to population density. How are different cities shaped, physically? The display contrasts a relatively low-density, spread-out city like Los Angeles, with a high-density, compact city such as Hong Kong. The display shows different trends in city planning in three-dimensional form.

Increasing Resilience invites you to choose a virtual city based on one of a number of different landscapes – desert, say, or coastal. What steps might you take to future-proof 'your' city? Real case studies from around the world are fed into the display to provide comparisons.

The zone communicates that urban planning is about achieving balance and taking account of the interrelationships between different parts of the city. Placed centrally in the exhibition, adjacent to Go Electric, Keep Moving, Smart Buildings and Safe and Sound, this zone is a reminder of the central role of planning in creating and maintaining sustainable cities.

There is no logic that can be superimposed on the city; people make it, and it is to them, not buildings, that we must fit our plans.

Jane Jacobs.

Creating Cities

The forces of urbanization, of demographic and climate change are together putting huge pressures on the quality of life of citizens and the performance of the city economy. In this chapter, we will see how, through planning and careful management, cities can become more resilient to such forces securing the social, economic and natural capital of current citizens and future generations.

How are cities made?

Cities are built in the image of their cycle of production, distribution, exchange and consumption. The crystallization of this cycle into concrete urban form is what makes and remakes the built fabric of the city. At least, this was the understanding of 19th century social theorists who saw parts of cities dedicated to production and manufacturing, others to the movement of goods and finally parts dedicated to mass consumption such as the department stores that were emerging in 19th century Paris. Over time, what became apparent was that cities were actually made in the image of the predominant technological revolution of their age. In the industrial revolution, cities were shaped by the emergence of factories around which residential communities were being built. In the age of railways, cities opened up to their countryside and nations were centralised around their capital cities through radial rail networks. In the age of steel, new technologies allowed cities to grow vertically and in the age of mass production and the car, cities expanded horizontally with the creation of suburbs. Finally, the age of information technology allowed cities to become more competitive in turning their 'services economy' truly global and the current green revolution is helping cities build more with less.

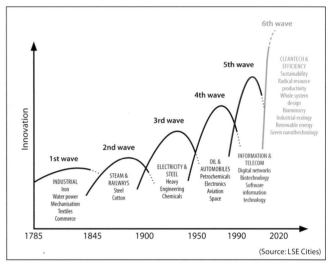

Waves of Technological Innovation.

Historically however, there are too many occasions when cities, that were left to the devices of market and technological forces alone or were reliant on one predominant mode of production, from mining to auto-making, perished or failed. It is the role of planners to correct these negative externalities of market forces and steer the future of cities into sustainable paths.

In London, former redundant dockyards have been redeveloped into mixed use neighborhoods.

Barcelona's growth around an urban grid has helped integrate the city, rather than promote the growth of separate districts.

The need for broadbased planning

Today's planners have come a long way since their utopian counterparts of the early and mid 20th century, whose indicators of successful transformations were based on narrow terms such as health and overcrowding. Rather than relying on utopian visions of the future, where the city was subdivided into rational districts for living and working to improve the health of citizens, today we understand that cities must respond to many more dimensions of life, which are often interdependent and from which we must fit our plans.

Yet, the pressures of rapid urbanization in Asia are putting these earlier lessons from Europe and North America to the test, partly because we are still mis-measuring the lives of our citizens. Building new housing blocks to accommodate households that were in vulnerable areas only deals with one aspect of people's lives, mainly their physical capital. A new approach of 'broad-based planning' that measures success on the environmental, social and economic performance of today's and tomorrow's cities is at the heart of this revolution that is often referred to as sustainable planning.

Modernist planners such as those behind the building of Brasilia subdivided the city according to use, taking away some of the vitality of mixed use cities.

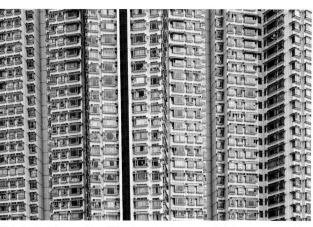

High density living provides efficiencies such as lower costs for infrastructure provision.

21

I've always believed that if you can't measure it, you can't manage it.

Michael R. Bloomberg, Mayor of New York City.

What are sustainable cities?

For cities to flourish, households and businesses need the necessary levels of capital to help them reach their desired goals. This capital is multidimensional and may be subdivided into physical assets (such as infrastructure and shelter), social assets (such as one's supporting social networks), natural assets (access to resources water and green areas), financial assets (money or other liquid assets) and finally human ones (education and skills).

These types of assets are threatened by shocks such as economic downturns, seasonality, natural disasters and resource fluctuations. Planners can lower the vulnerabilities of these capital assets by looking at the latest information on key threats and maintain assets at the right levels. Measuring assets and

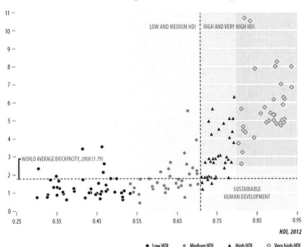

Ecological footprint, 2007 (global hectares per capita)

Note: Ecological footprint is a measure of the biocapacity of the earth and the demand on biocapacity. It depends on the average productivity of biologically productive land and water in a given year.

Source: HDRO calculations and Global Footprint Netwrok (2011)

managing threats is at the heart of the sustainable city, which is being shaped today.

From measurement to form

Planners are on the quest for the truly sustainable city that provides economic opportunities and high living standards for all its citizens, all within a city's environmental limits. There are certain cities that do it better than others and these have important physical characteristics.

Mixed use cities provide opportunities for interactions amongst different social groups and promote the positive economic externalities of living close together.

Zurich. Mixed use cities provide opportunities for economic spillovers and exchange which are at the heart of the new economy.

Planning powers such as mixed use zoning that keep activities together rather than zoning them out, allow for positive interactions between different sectors in the economy.

A further sustainable planning approach involves the promotion of high density urban environments that can be better served with health, energy and transport infrastructure compared to low density sprawling cities. Planning powers that allow minimum density development around transport nodes promote both economic efficiencies as well decrease congestion and poor air quality.

Moscow is expanding its territory to the south west, with the development of high density transport oriented centers surrounded by green areas.

In the first part of this chapter, our view was of cities being made out of the crystallization of economic and technological patterns of their time. Today, planners are seeing their policies turned into urban forms known as eco-towns that take some of the ideas of broad-based planning into physical reality. The challenge, however remains trying to make such forms accessible to all levels of society.

We are the masterplanners

A city cannot be successful if its sustainability is based on economic and environmental parameters alone. The social dimension of sustainability that opens the city's opportunities to as many citizens as possible requires progressive planning approaches that break physical boundaries that reinforce economic inequalities.

Sao Paulo is trying to connect its formal and informal settlements, which are currently divided by strong boundaries.

City planners who can take advantage of economic boom cycles by creating the necessary planning gain instruments as in the case of North American cities or providing subsidized affordable housing from private development as in the case of London is one way that cities can provide benefits to both high and lower income groups. More importantly, the role of planners is being reversed. From the modernist definition of the planner as a master-builder determining the future of citizens, we see new participatory planning approaches in a range of cities from Brazil to Germany allowing urbanites to determine the priorities of their cities future.

Allowing today's citizens to measure themselves and plan for their future does not, however, take away from the role of the planner, who must also represent the interests of future generations.

London planners are planning for the future, with their biggest challenge to increase housing supply and affordability in the city.

This chapter has looked at the forces behind the making of cities and the role of today's planners in guiding the interests of citizens and businesses to sustainable futures. From the modernist and rational master planning of the early 20th century, today's planners use a broader information base to measure the success of their cities and take a more participatory and holistic approach to city challenges. Nowhere is this holistic approach more evident than in future public transport decisions that work at the largest scale of the city and that can impact the city's economic performance through travel time gains, improve its air quality and provide better integration between poorer and wealthier parts of the city. This is the focus of the next chapter.

NO

CO

The future of city
transport is electric.

KEEP
MOVING

Who's at
the wheel?

If you come to Keep Moving from Safe and Sound, you'll be aware that a streamlined transport system is essential for keeping our cities safe. Keep Moving also shares the cityscape floor graphic with Creating Cities, a reminder that transport is one of the most important components of urban planning. The challenges represented in this zone relate to the creation of suitable transport networks to meet cities' needs, as well as the development of low carbon transport options that won't add to the problem of pollution.

The zone design is influenced by the linearity of roads, lines and tracks, while the graphics reflect the ways in which travel information is displayed. Curving structures moving through the displays represent the myriad networks running through our cities; text runs in ribbons along the curves.

The attractor display is a helix-shaped sculpture representing people and vehicles streaming into a city; the more people, the more the city becomes congested, resulting in a tangled snarl at the center. The ultimate goal for city planners is to achieve complete mobility (as opposed to the snarl) and the displays and interactives illustrate the challenges but also the solutions that might make this possible.

Just as no two cities are the same, no two have exactly the same transport requirements. The bike, bus, train or tram? activity invites you to plan the right mix of transport options for different types of cities. Should there be an underground? A light rail? A commuter rail system? A bus network?

Complete Mobility gives us a seductive view of integrated travel-planning in the future. A phone app will allow us to plan

and pay for our travel (working like a kind of travel card), inform us of any changes and facilitate changing from network to network, whether trains, buses, planes, smart cars … The exciting thing about this is the fact that it's all within our grasp. Most of the technology already exists. Visitors are challenged in the interactive to take a journey through a city and see what a difference complete mobility makes.

A display of vehicles – a 'Boris bike', electric motorbike and e-car – reminds us of some of the sustainable transport options available to us now. The electric car is carefully located in the exhibition as it represents an important link between Keep Moving and Go Electric. The electric car has potential to act as a kind of mobile battery, charging during low demand times, storing energy and then returning the energy to the grid in times of peak demand.

*A developed country is not a place where the poor have cars,
it's where the rich ride public transportation.*

Enrique Peñalosa, Former Mayor of Bogotá.

Keep Moving

Given the overwhelmingly high rates of urbanization, one major challenge is how to tackle urban mobility and how to move citizens quickly, efficiently, and cleanly across cities.

In Beijing, the increase in traffic has led the city to develop a sophisticated public transportation network. With six million cars projected to be on Beijing's roads in 2016, this is the only way to keep the city moving.

By 2050, China is projected to have 900 million motor vehicles – more than the total number of cars, trucks, and motorcycles in the world today. At the current rate of motorization, 2.3 billion automobiles will be added worldwide by 2050, and more than 80 percent of them will end up on the roads and highways of developing countries. Two key reasons are the high rates of urbanization and a growing middle class. People will have the disposable income to buy cars. The challenge for these cities and city decision-makers will be to create a robust and efficient enough mass transit systems to deter citizens from using private vehicles. Policies need to encourage high density developments with a reliable public transportation system.

In Bangkok, traffic congestion led to the development of a Sky Rail solution that moves people through the city above the traffic.

We can see now in places like Jakarta, Mexico City and Bangkok, road congestion is one of the biggest concerns and issues in the city. Jakarta loses $3 billion per annum due to road congestion and based on current trends it is predicted that the city will reach total gridlock by 2014. In Beijing, the health costs from local air pollution are estimated at $3.5 billion annually. Such road congestion leads to decreased economic productivity, increased road deaths, energy consumption, air pollution, and poor health.

A defining characteristic of a city is its public transportation system and its level of connectivity. An efficient public transportation system consistently ranks as the top driver for attracting people to a city. It gives an urban area a competitive edge. The challenge is that mass transit systems often take

In Mexico City, traffic congestion has resulted in people spending several hours in their cars to get to work. The city is now seeking to reduce the problem by incentivizing people to use public transport.

decades to be fully realized and cannot keep pace with the rates of growth currently being experienced in many of the world's cities.

A primary responsibility for city planners is to develop and implement strong policies that expand and develop public transportation systems, while also implementing measures that deter car use. This requires policies that coordinate land-use planning and infrastructure development. Additionally, transport finances are often poured into road infrastructure and car parking facilities, which caters for private vehicle owners. Such investment needs to be balanced with the creation and enhancement of public transport networks if we are to avoid the negative impacts of under occupied cars blocking our cities roads and contributing to hazardous air pollution.

Convenience is a top priority for people today. To incentivize people to use public transport, there must be supporting mechanisms which allow for integration. Route integration is critical for users, ensuring that they can plan a journey from start to finish on reliable and efficient public transport. Regularity of service is also critical to allow people to travel at all times of day, and in addition, providing integrated ticketing creates simplicity and convenience which is critical to ensuring people make the shift from their cars to the public network. Comfort and affordability will also be a consideration for transport users particularly when they are used to the space and privacy of their cars.

Investment can also be used for transport demand management including mechanisms such as congestion charging, tolling, and low emissions zones. These traffic management schemes are designed to reduce congestion but also raise awareness in road users about the harmful impacts of air pollution from vehicle movements. However, these systems will not be successful if there is not a suitable public transportation alternative.

London is greening its bus network, further reducing the environmental impact of transport.

There is also an opportunity, and a need, to develop transit oriented development. A transit system will only be as good as the number of people who use it. Transport networks must be fully integrated and embedded into a city and made more desirable than using private vehicles. It is defined as 'any development, macro or micro, that is focused around a transit node, and facilitates complete ease of access to the transit facility, thereby inducing people to prefer to walk and use public transportation over personal modes of transport'. Providing transit oriented developments along metro lines that can move large numbers very quickly can help keep the city moving and deliver people from home to work in times that do not impinge their quality of life. Proving above ground solutions such as dedicated road lanes for electrically powered bus rapid transit (eBRT) provides a secondary system that can reach into the wider arteries of the city providing greater land coverage and links into the main network. Converging these different forms of transportation at transport hubs allows easy transition from one mode to another, making journeys quicker, and simpler to plan. Cycle schemes, pedestrian routes, water taxis and light rail solutions are all viable solutions for city transport and an integrated network will ensure their success.

Amsterdam

Tram in Berlin

Traffic in Beijing

A sustainable transport system brings together social, economic and environmental benefits.

Transit oriented developments are key to limiting urban sprawl, reducing congestion, and lowering greenhouse gas emissions. It is more expensive and more difficult to deliver an efficient public transport system in cities with low densities and sprawl. This is why intelligent urban planning is crucial in delivering a strong mass transit plan. City policymakers must plan for mixed-use, high density, polycentric cities. Some urban areas, given their limited land space, have had to grow upwards e.g. Hong Kong and Singapore. Hong Kong has a very high density, an extensive public transport system, and subsequently one of the highest public transit modal shares in the world. Furthermore, experiences show that well-designed developments not only increases ridership of public transit by drawing more travelers out of cars and into trains and buses, it can also serve as a hub for organising community development and revitalising long-distressed urban districts. They offer environmental, social and economic benefits.

Good public transportation systems are the backbone of a city and have the ability to attract international investment which can regenerate and revitalise a city. This critical infrastructure needs efficient management and as a valuable city asset should be protected from failure, and provide its users with a safe and secure journey as they make their way across the city. Keeping the city safe is the focus of the next chapter.

Mumbai

Having a real fire in the exhibition wouldn't be very sustainable, so we 'lock-in' a safe fire inside the Safe & Sound word walls.

Dan Savage, Exhibition Designer, Event Communications.

CARE SH

SENS

SENS

PEACE

SUSTAI

24/
7/

Protecting
the City

The fire triangle. Remove just one element – oxygen, fuel or heat – to stop fires.

70% of companies that suffer a major fire never reopen.

Safe and Sound forms a bridge between Smart Buildings and Keep Moving, reflecting the fact that the rise of urbanization and connectivity has a downside. Our cities face bigger safety and security risks than ever before. City planners are constantly at work to find and address these risks, ensuring our safety.

Walls wrap around the Safe and Sound zone, giving a feeling of security. Words representing well-being are cut out on the attractor walls: 'reassurance', 'sense', 'trust', 'peace of mind'. Viewing through the cutouts, you'll see illustrations by a Finnish artist, which depict all topics covered in Safe and Sound, from natural disasters to crime. These images connect to moving images on a number of screens within the zone which reflect the same themes.

Also visible through the protective layer of words is a fire, representing one of the major threats to any city.

All of these elements appear to be locked in by the vault-like structure of the façade.

Once inside the enclosed zone, the design language is inspired by data visualization – for example, satellite images overlaid with graphics picking out key facts and figures. Display screens embedded in the walls show 'live' feeds of different aspects of the city, painting a high-tech, continuously evolving picture. The space is light and bright, light being an important tool in keeping city streets safe.

Exhibits within the zone look at individual security challenges, from fire, through incident response, to crowd control. One of the most popular interactives is the Access Control test, putting visitors in the role of a person checking ID badges against live faces. How good is your facial recognition? Better than a computer?

The introduction to the zone lists some of the potential threats to our cities, including fire, road accidents, crime, terrorism, natural disasters. But these threats are paired with a display profiling the people and services that work 24/7 to prevent, detect, respond, recover.

Rapid Response is a software interactive that places you in the role of the emergency services – fire, police, ambulance. One visitor 'designs' an emergency, choosing the type and location, while the other visitor – who acts as the despatcher – has to decide how best to respond.

Where possible (and appropriate) interactives have a fun and amusing approach – in keeping with the reassuring and uplifting tone of the zone.

Out of this nettle, danger, we pluck this flower, safety.

Henry IV, William Shakespeare.

Safe & Sound

The three megatrends explored in the Forces of Change chapter bring specific challenges for cities in terms of protecting both people and assets. As more people move to cities and the world becomes better connected, safety and security risks increase. Flooding, earthquakes, landslides, acts of terror, traffic accidents, crime and fires are some of the challenges faced by cities across the world. Protecting people, property and infrastructure is central to the successful functioning of any city.

As more people move to cities security risks increase.

There are four main approaches to providing safety and security in cities – prevention, detection, response and recovery. These measures are crucial in protecting key services and infrastructure, keeping people safe and ensuring cities can operate as business centres.

Surveillance systems can assist in identifying, responding to and investigating incidents.

The approaches to public safety in cities are not new. A London doctor, John Snow was the first person to make the link between contaminated water supply and cholera. During a cholera epidemic in Soho, London in 1854 he plotted a map of the incidents of cholera against the location of water pumps in the area. Using the map he was able to convince the local authorities to remove the handle from a pump, where the water supply had become contaminated by a cesspool – the cause of the outbreak. Conventional wisdom at the time was that cholera was caused by 'miasma' – a foul, poisonous air. By using data, Dr Snow was able to detect the cause of the epidemic and ultimately prevent its spread.

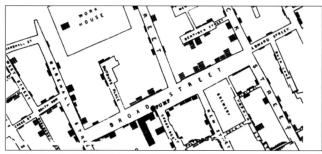

Dr John Snow showed the link between cholera and contaminated water supply through mapping in 1854.

The use of technology can help city planners to take measures to reduce risk and also respond to them more quickly and effectively when they occur. Prevention protects people and infrastructure as early as possible; this can be achieved through the active management of risks to safety and security. For example intelligent traffic management control systems now make it easier for cities to keep traffic moving, reduce congestion and road traffic accidents. 20 percent of all road crashes are from secondary crashes caused by congestion following a previous accident. The likelihood of a secondary crash increases by almost three percent for every minute the first crash remains a hazard.

Managing traffic through control systems can reduce exposure to air pollutants and reduce accidents.

When disasters strike they can cause widespread panic — whether it is fireworks being set off into a crowd at a football match or a fire at a train station, nightclub or hotel. Understanding the dynamics of crowds and how they react to events can be used to plan more effectively, recognise threats and head off disasters.

Technology can help keep us safe in city environments. By modelling crowd behavior, decision makers can predict where and when a critical situation may arise. Such modelling can help architects plan safer buildings — say a stadium, airport or exhibition centers. By using models, simple procedures and plans can be implemented to prevent many disasters happening. Equally, it can be used by decision makers to make real-time decisions when large crowds are being managed. Using models of how crowds behave, decision makers can understand what will happen if an intervention is not made. This allows crowds to be more effectively managed, for example by opening doors, or giving warnings to crowds to prevent accidents happening.

In London, crowd control is essential to allowing people to move quickly and safely around transport hubs.

Technology also plays a part in preventing and detecting crime. Intelligent surveillance and CCTV can help identify possible incidents, allow emergency services to respond and also look through footage to aid investigations following an incident. Face recognition or license plate recognition can be used to enhance security at sensitive sites such as airports or enforce regulations in cities such as the congestion zone in London. Surveillance systems have been found to reduce crime in parking lots by 51 percent and by 23 percent on public transportation.

Responding to accidents and emergencies is complex and involves many organisations. Technology can help in ensuring that emergency services can continue their operations, reach incidents rapidly, share information between agencies and develop effective responses. Over-stretched, uncoordinated and overloaded communications systems all hampered the emergency responses to terrorist attacks in New York, London and Madrid. For example in Madrid each emergency service had different communication technologies and systems. Equally in New York, many fire fighters died when the Twin Towers collapsed as they were unable to receive the warnings that police officers had received from police helicopters at the scene. Cities are now putting in place effective technology to enable responses to be coordinated from command and control centers, using the same systems.

Coordinated responses from control centers are essential to responding effectively to emergencies.

The Neues Museum in Berlin restoration included reliable and fault proof power distribution. It also has high-quality building and safety technology for increased safety and security to protect the museum's valuable exhibits, and visitors and staff.

Through designing resilience into city systems and infrastructure, cities can ensure that where parts of systems are affected by disasters they can be isolated from the remainder of the city's infrastructure to avoid total failure. Resilient, smart grid networks for example can remotely isolate areas of failure on the electricity grid – whilst allowing systems to continue in other areas. The role of buildings in our cities energy demand is the focus of the next chapter.

The continuity of operations and information sharing is crucial to allowing recovery to happen from disasters. City systems need to be resilient and able to continue in times of stress. It is essential for example that clean water supplies are protected as well as electricity supply to allow a rapid and effective response, without this recovery is hampered and disasters can become greater in scale quickly.

Cities like Madrid have implemented coordination centers to ensure the quick and integrated dispatch of responders to emergency situations.

Resilient city infrastructure is important in allowing cities to respond to disasters.

It is a fantastic building, really astonishing but I think what's in it is even more important … for developing good city plans all over the world.

Rita Ottervik, Mayor of Trondheim, Norway.

SMART BUILDINGS

The Smart Buildings zone sits between Creating Cities and Safe and Sound. The design of the Smart Buildings zone shares its DNA with Creating Cities, which makes sense given they're both about planning and designing physical structures.

Urban-dwellers spend, on average, 90 percent of their time in buildings. Therefore our quality of life depends on designing better and smarter buildings. The key message of the Smart Buildings zone is that we should plan and design our buildings holistically.

Forming one boundary of the zone, you'll notice a display dedicated to the design of the Crystal. That's because sustainable building principles were applied to every aspect of the building. The exhibit demonstrates just why the Crystal deserves to be called 'smart', with a live tally of the building's day-to-day sustainability, for example the amount of energy generated by

the building's ground source heat pump and its solar thermal system, or how much of the water consumed on a given day was provided by the black water recycling system.

The building design team and the building itself were filmed during the design and construction of the Crystal to paint a picture of just what was involved in the design of this unique facility. Back of house areas not normally accessible to the public are opened up in the film and discussed in detail to provide a deeper level of knowledge about the process of sustainable building design.

Another exhibit presents the multiplicity of building types in a city and asks, how can buildings be more efficient? All of the variables, from passive temperature control, to using renewable materials, are discussed. You're invited to get hands-on with a display showcasing different types of building material, itemizing their pros and cons.

Moving through the zone, you enter a tunnel of graphic lightboxes. The graphics take inspiration from design sketches and blueprints, while a series of audio points offers different perspectives on designing smart buildings from architects, engineers and urban planners.

Smart buildings are responsive buildings and the design reflects this. Just as buildings communicate with environment, the exhibit communicates with visitors. One of the key messages is communicated in Change Your Behavior. This display looks at how we could use buildings more efficiently, for example by working from home.

Create Your Own Sustainable Building is a software-based interactive inviting you to apply the principles of sustainability to your own design. Do you have to compromise aesthetics to achieve maximum sustainability, or can you have it all? Unlock your inner architect …

A house is a machine for living in.

Le Corbusier.

Smart Building

After centuries when buildings only had to provide security and shelter, we are now in a period with scarce natural resources which also requires energy and water efficiency from buildings and our expectations as a building user have evolved in line with the digital age that we have now entered.

Buildings through time
Buildings animate the city landscape giving form to culture and a home to communities. They are representations of a city's aspirations through time.

Historically cities emerged next to waterways allowing for the transportation of commodities, creating powerful trading centres and resulting in great wealth for its inhabitants. That wealth was often invested in the buildings as symbols of power and status, and many of those amazing architectural creations can still be witnessed today in the oldest cities in the world. Places of worship were often at the heart of the city, and became monuments to its power and success.

Hagia Sophia, built in the sixth century AD first as a church then converted to a mosque, was a monument to the power of Constantinople and the wealth it generated being at the heart of the east-west trading route. Today it continues to be the symbol of Istanbul, an emerging megacity, with its continental link between Europe and Asia.

Many of the buildings in cities represented the surrounding activities with large warehouses next to waterways, and homes providing shelter and security for workers, and also buildings which housed the key functions of city administration. Today,

Hagia Sophia – a historic monument to the power of Constantinople, past and present.

buildings are also designed to offer a lifestyle ideal that goes beyond function and purpose resulting in an increased demand for scarce resources.

Building Design
We can learn a huge amount from the architects, designers and constructors of the past looking at their approach to building form and how building design responded both to the activities of those who occupied it, but also to its surrounding environment, climate and weather. It is still evident today that the original street layouts in Ho Chi Minh City were oriented to the prevailing winds, allowing air movement to pass through the space uninterrupted, creating a cooling effect along the city streets. In hot climates, excessive solar gain was limited through wall thicknesses, the use of appropriate materials and natural shading, and in cold climates, animal waste was used to insulate

buildings in winter and used as fuel as the climate became warmer, thereby reducing the insulation around the building as it was no longer needed. Lighting was provided by natural sources, either through building design or fire. People also used space differently, responding to daylight cycles - working during hours of light, and sleeping during hours of darkness. People gathered in one space when heat and light was needed, rather than our occupancy patterns of today, as people crave a need for private space in our crowded city lives.

However, the buildings in our cities today are very different. Some continue to be exotic symbols of prosperity, and others, including post war responses to housing shortages which were built in the midst of austerity with limited resources, are built to provide a certain function, neither approach puts environmental consideration at the forefront of design.

The growing demand for energy

Building design often follows current trends, as does the use of particular materials in construction, and now, our desire for taller buildings and our need for increased density of housing has led us to using much newer materials such as steel and concrete providing the necessary structural stability, and glass, allowing for lightweight construction reducing impact on the structure, giving what is perceived to be a desirable aesthetic finish. Each of these materials undergoes an energy intensive production process, responds differently to climatic conditions and provides a specific response to thermal conductivity which has to be managed by installed mechanical or electrical building systems.

The move to energy intensive methods of heating and cooling our buildings, and to lighting has resulted in rising global demands for energy resources, largely delivered by fossil fuels. These basic needs account for approximately 40 percent of global energy consumption. As well as mineral and resource depletion, heavy extraction and energy generation processes have led to high levels of greenhouse gas production which is the primary contributor to climate change. As global population increases and more buildings are constructed, there will be an increasing demand on energy resources to meet basic needs, and as wealth improves in developing countries, there will also be a growing demand for energy intensive domestic appliances and electronics. Consumer electronics and computer

equipment currently represent 15 percent of residential energy consumption and this is expected to triple 2030.

In Singapore, more sophisticated building controls allow for power and lighting to shut off at night when spaces are unused. As a result, automated systems can result in huge energy savings.

The systems we install in our buildings need to be as efficient and as clean as possible to reduce unnecessary energy consumption and we need to be smarter in how we manage our energy use.

The London skyline is the epitome of building design culture displaying the powerhouse that is its central business district.

Managing our energy needs

The future of building energy management lies in the ability to use smart technologies to optimise a building's energy use. Building automation systems can integrate the energy uses within a building to ensure that consumption is limited to absolute need and responds to the patterns of occupancy. Having the ability to control the internal environment so that heat or cool air generated from buildings systems is not lost to the external space requires tightly sealed buildings. Where this exists, building automation systems can regulate the use of energy much more precisely and ensure that the internal comfort levels are maintained. Heat can be reused, and recycled between systems reducing the energy requirements. Thermal systems can respond more accurately to the external temperatures, and humidity and air flow can be managed to ensure that the internal air quality and comfort is maintained. Lighting can also be controlled dynamically to respond to occupancy and to the levels of daylight entering into a space which allows for optimal response rather than using pre-set lighting levels throughout the day. This is particularly useful in offices and other working spaces where certain levels of lighting are required and where lighting levels vary significantly throughout the day.

Modern design needs to ensure that the internal heat of a building is not lost through windows, ensuring that resources are not wasted through thermal losses.

Media Harbour in Dusseldorf combines old and new buildings with the highest standards of technology infrastructure to accommodate the modern media industry.

Managing our buildings in this way allows the monitoring of energy consumption. Large spikes in energy use can be identified and these irregularities can be eliminated through efficient control systems. These systems also have the capability of monitoring the building systems and locating faults and maintenance needs, even before they occur.

By understanding building energy use and optimising building systems through intelligent and energy efficiently technology, there is the potential to reduce energy consumption by 50 percent. If all our new and existing buildings could integrate smart technology, we could significantly reduce total global energy consumption.

With a rising awareness worldwide of the impacts of energy consumption and its negative effects on the climate, governments are now introducing policy and regulation to limit the wasteful consumption of energy and to seek design alternatives to energy intensive buildings. Cities are also developing their own initiatives to reduce energy consumption from their building stock, with challenging targets for carbon reductions. They are acting upon the need to manage energy and move from the building scale to a neighborhood scale to reduce wastage in distribution. By acting to reduce energy wastage through buildings and their distribution networks, cities are becoming flagships in the fight against climate change.

The roof of the Sony Centre in Berlin has been designed to moderate light, and maintain internal comfort levels, limiting the use of power in its operations.

Kuala Lumpur

The need to rethink the way we supply of power to buildings is as big a challenge as reducing their consumption, if not bigger, given the complex technologies involved. This is the focus of the next chapter.

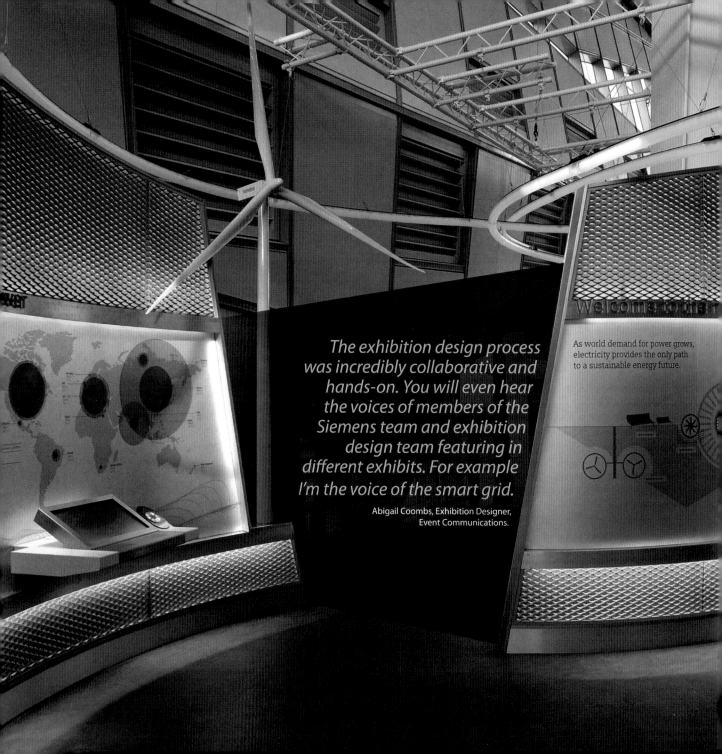

The exhibition design process was incredibly collaborative and hands-on. You will even hear the voices of members of the Siemens team and exhibition design team featuring in different exhibits. For example I'm the voice of the smart grid.

Abigail Coombs, Exhibition Designer,
Event Communications.

As world demand for power grows, electricity provides the only path to a sustainable energy future.

GO ELECTRIC

Go Electric is located between the Keep Moving and Water is Life zones and illustrates the technologies that are helping to make renewable energy cheaper, more efficient and more widely available. Given this is an exhibit about electricity, two of the key design ideas are 'attracting' and 'challenging'. Displays invite visitors in and then challenge them with the issues around powering our cities. Within the zone there's a push/pull relationship between Area 1 - formulaic, structured, rigid elements (representing traditional approaches to electricity generation) and Area 2 - an organic, flexible, pliable network (representing the smart grid of the New Electricity Age).

The city grid is represented in this zone by the overhead web of illuminated cables. They, along with the glowing panels at the base of the display structures, create a sense of warmth and light in the zone – reminding us of two of the most important functions

You don't get much more real and sensational than live electricity pulsing through the space!

Steve Simons, Creative Director, Event Communications.

of electricity. Designing the light lines was a major challenge involving theatrical lighting designers and programmers and a specialist rigging/hanging company to suspend the installation in the air.

One of the most spectacular elements of the whole exhibition is the Tesla coil. The exhibit encourages visitors to think about energy supply and demand by matching their physical movements to the demand for electricity. When demand is high, intense physical movement is required to trigger the Tesla coil. The installation shows that supply and demand is always in flux.

Life Depends on Energy is a display wall exploring different power sources.

Graphics, objects and models set into the wall emphasize the need for renewable and sustainable sources of energy, explaining why we can no longer rely on fossil fuels for our energy needs.

Other displays include Banking Energy, an interactive that examines how electricity is stored, Get the Balance Right, a display that shows how we can make better use of the energy we have (and, potentially, make a profit!), Energy Near and Far, which explains that energy supplies will need to be more integrated in the future to manage centralized and decentralized power supply.

*The growth of clean energy can lead to the growth of our economy,
The closer we get to this new energy future, the harder the opposition
is going to fight, it's a debate between looking backwards and looking
forward, between those who are ready to seize the future and those
who are afraid of the future.*

Barack Obama, President of the United States of America, 2009.

Go Electric

Our cities require energy to function, to power, heat and cool our buildings, as a fuel for transport, to produce food or to communicate and share information. Energy is involved in everything we do. The last chapter looked at how buildings can be designed and operated intelligently to maximize their efficiency and reduce their emissions of greenhouse gases.

In Berlin, Energy Saving Partnerships have reduced emissions of CO_2 from 1,300 buildings.

This chapter looks in more detail at the challenges of meeting energy demand and some of the technologies to help us manage energy supply and distribution effectively. It specifically looks at the challenges around electricity generation and supply. As with other city challenges, the megatrends of increasing population in cities mean that the demand for energy in cities is growing. At the same time climate change means we need to rethink how we provide and use energy. Energy has to be supplied and used more sustainably to reduce its impact on climate change and local air quality. CO_2 emissions from fossil fuels generating electricity are increasing and reached a historic high of 31.6 gigatonnes in 2012. At the same time our energy also needs to be affordable for people and businesses. Energy is a global commodity and price fluctuations can impact significantly on economies.

Fossil fuels provide 80 percent of our energy at the moment.

Increasing demand for energy

Demand for energy continues to grow. Global energy consumption doubled from 4,000 million tonnes of energy in 1971 to just over 8,000 million tonnes in 2010. It is set to grow by another 40 percent by 2035. Fossil fuels count for 80 percent of primary energy (Oil 32.4 percent, Coal 27.3 percent and Gas 21.4 percent). The remainder is provided by nuclear (5.7 percent), hydro (2.3 percent), biofuels and waste (10 percent). Geothermal, solar, wind and heat make up 0.9 percent. Fossil fuels will continue to provide 75 percent of our energy in 2035, the proportion of nuclear remains the same and renewables are expected to grow rapidly.

The rapid increase in electricity demand

The global demand for electricity is growing at twice the rate of global energy consumption. By 2035 global demand for energy will reach 32,000 terawatt hours, a growth of 70 per cent compared to 2010. The challenge of meeting this demand is made harder as around a third of old power stations will be shut down over that period. To meet global electricity demand in 2035, 5,890 gigawatts of capacity additions are needed. This is greater than the world's total installed capacity at the moment.

In 2010 coal was the principal fuel used to generate electricity (41 percent) followed by gas (22 percent).

Renewables accounted for 20 percent and nuclear 13 percent. By 2035 renewables will account for 31 percent of the generation mix. Gas and coal will continue to be an important fuel for electricity. The investment challenge in the power sector between now and 2035 is $16.9 trillion.

In Tokyo, a cap and trade program is being used to reduce emissions. So far 23 percent savings have been made.

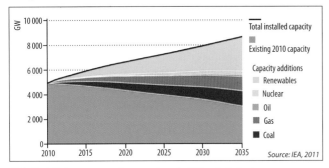

Global installed power generation capacity and additions by technology.

Smart grids

The way in which we provide electricity from generation plant to consumers will need to change in future cities. Not only is demand for electricity growing but the way it is being used is changing. Electricity is playing an increasing role in providing heat to buildings and in fuelling vehicles in cities. In addition the change in the electricity mix, with more renewable sources that generate power intermittently such as wind and solar, means

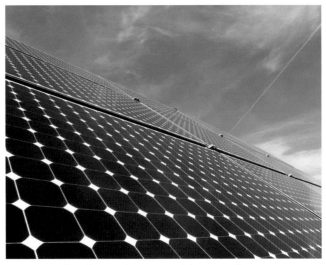

By 2035 renewables will account for 31 percent of electricity production.

that more active management of the electricity grid is needed to match supply with demand, and store electricity on the grid at times when it is not needed. Electric vehicles for example could be used to store electricity at times when the grid is over-supplying or it could be converted to hydrogen, for use as a fuel or converted back to electricity when it is needed.

Conventional electricity grids are linear. They take power from large, centralised power stations, often located remotely from urban areas via high-voltage transmission lines to demand centers, where it is supplied via distribution lines to homes and workplaces. This approach is inefficient - in effect far more electricity is generated than is actually needed, to ensure uninterrupted power supply. This approach is also unresponsive to the changing electricity needs above.

Electricity grids of the future – smart grids will integrate and enhance new grid technologies with renewable energy generation, storage, increased customer participation, better communication, sensors, meters and computation. They will provide for the two-way flow of electricity and information, where consumers can also become producers of electricity. They will deliver real-time information that will allow for real-time automated balancing of supply with demand. Distributed sources of electricity generation will also utilize the heat produced from the production of electricity to heat and cool buildings locally.

Smart grids will ensure better security, quality and reliability of power. They will be more efficient, meaning less electricity will need to be generated to meet demand. They will also reduce the environmental impact of the supply of electrical power and heating/cooling to cities. IT systems based on real-time data will allow for flexible tariffs and provide transparency over the costs and savings for consumers.

Electricity is playing a greater role in fueling vehicles.

In Copenhagen, the government is aiming for the City to be the first carbon neutral capital by 2025.

WATER IS LIFE

The vision was to have real water in the exhibition, but we knew it would be a challenge. We had an expert team working on the engineering, and calculating how to have six tonnes of water continuously flowing. Happily, the final result is just as we dreamed it.

Dan Savage, Exhibition Designer, Event Communications.

Water is Life overlaps with Go Electric and Healthy Life, a reminder that water is both an important source of energy and an essential resource for sustaining human life. Access to clean drinking water is one of the most pressing global challenges. Although water covers 75 percent of the planet's surface, only 2.5 percent of the planet's water supply is freshwater (the rest is seawater) and of that, only 0.75 percent is easily accessible.

The stunning water feature illustrates this conundrum. The water flows down into a tank, some of it spilling over the sides, seemingly wasted. The tank represents the total amount of water on earth, communicating just how little water is available to support the seven billion people on the planet.

The design language is, appropriately, watery. Text panels form the wall supporting the waterfall and content appears to ripple behind the sheet of water.

Displays look at different ways of improving water efficiency, from harvesting rainwater to making seawater drinkable. The Water Footprint activity tallies our individual water consumption (the average person in London uses 158 litres per day) and explores ways of reducing it.

Drinking From the Ocean is a software interactive that takes you through the steps of making seawater drinkable. Case studies illustrate where and how desalination is happening around the world.

Harvesting the Rain is a mesmerizing film that shows how easy it would be to harvest rainwater. In fact, harvested rainwater is used to supply all the water used in the attractor display!

Put a Plug in it illustrates how much water is lost due to leaks in the system. These leaks are often caused by ageing pipes. The content takes you through the strategies and solutions available to city water managers to ensure as little water as possible is lost.

Anyone who can solve the problems of water will be worthy of two Nobel prizes - one for peace and one for science.

John F. Kennedy.

Water is Life

Water is essential to life. Water is not just used to drink, to grow food, to cook and to clean. It is an integral raw material in many of the products we make and processes we need to support our daily lives. For example water is essential in the production of electricity. It is used in the extraction, transportation and processing of fossil fuels. The production of biofuels, relies on the irrigation of crops. The IEA estimate that water withdrawals for energy production alone in 2010 were 583 billion cubic meters globally. For energy alone the projected rise in water consumption could rise by 85 percent by 2035.

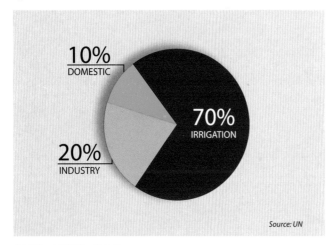

Source: UN

Breakdown of freshwater use.

The competition for water

Water is a vital and yet unevenly distributed resource. Canada has plenty of water, whilst Mexico, Pakistan, South Africa, most countries in North Africa and the Middle East suffer from frequent shortages. Even within countries such as India, China and Brazil, some regions have abundant supplies of fresh water whilst others are affected by drought. Just 2.5 percent of the 1.4 billion km^3 of water on the planet is fresh water. Only one percent of all fresh water is available for humans and ecosystems.

70 percent of freshwater is used in irrigation.

Given the need for water and its uneven distribution, it is no surprise that water resources are keenly contested. Between 1950 and 2000 the UN estimate that there were over 1,800 water conflicts over transboundary basins.

Cities face many challenges in providing access to water for their citizens.

Pressure on water supplies is only going to increase. As the world's population continues to grow, so the demand for fresh water increases. As the world population becomes more urbanized the demand in cities also grows and with it the need for wastewater treatment. UNESCO estimate that 80 percent of waste water is not collected or treated, the main source of this pollution is urban areas.

Globally, 80 percent of waste water is not collected for treatment, mainly in urban areas.

Climate change and water

Climate change will also impact on our access to fresh water. Variations in temperature and rainfall could impact water availability and increase the frequency and severity of flooding events, as well as disrupting ecosystems and man-made systems that maintain water quality. The UN Development Programme estimates that an increase of global temperatures of 3-4°C will force an additional 1.8 billion people to live in a water scarce environment by 2080 and two thirds of the world's population to live in areas of water stress.

Climate change could lead to two thirds of the world's population living in areas of water stress.

Managing our water

Cities face many different challenges in providing access to water. Their geographic location and available technologies play a part in determining where supplies come from and the distances required to provide them. For example groundwater aquifers provide 20 percent of water to those living in arid and semi-arid regions. But these regions receive limited or seasonal recharge making them susceptible to rapid depletion. The Northern Sahara Basin was exploited at almost twice its replenishment rate in the 1990s, causing many of its springs to stop flowing.

Cities face challenges in providing fresh water and ensuring they do not pollute water systems.

Even where groundwater supplies are meeting demand in cities, major problems can be caused by unregulated groundwater exploitation, and the disposal of solid and liquid wastes above or into these aquifers. A growing number of these aquifers are facing pollution from organic chemicals, pesticides, nitrates, heavy metals and waterborne pathogens. The level of water and wastewater service provision can also radically alter aquifer replenishment mechanisms, affecting not only the dynamic equilibrium between increased recharge availability and pumped withdrawals, but also the magnitude of the pollutant load and the rate of aquifer contamination. All these problems occur, to a certain degree, in towns and cities, depending on their type of groundwater supply.

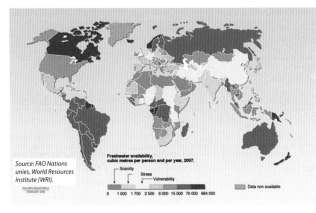

Source: FAO Nations unies, World Resources Institute (WRI).

Freshwater availability.

Given these challenges, cities have to employ innovative and efficient ways to manage water. A number of technologies and systems are available to achieve this such as rainwater harvesting and black and grey-water recycling. Cities must upgrade their water infrastructure and implement policies and protocols to reduce water pollution and reduce leakage. Land-use planning will also have to be integrated with water management.

Rainwater harvesting can play an important role in helping cities meet their water needs. It allows water to be collected and treated to drinking water standard. In Indian cities such as Chennai, Bangalore and Delhi rainwater harvesting is now happening on a large scale. Despite these cities receiving good levels of rainfall, it occurs during short spells of high intensity.

This pattern of rain means if it is not captured it flows rapidly away with little replenishment of groundwater. This can also lead to flash flooding. Rainwater harvesting not only helps to capture more of this water, but can help alleviate the risks of flooding.

In Delhi, rainwater harvesting is used on a large scale to capture water.

Cities need to rethink how they manage their wastewater. At the moment it is treated as a waste, to be flushed away and dealt with in large treatment works. However, wastewater can be recycled just like solid waste. It can be used for irrigation, household cleaning and flushing toilets. With additional treatment it can be used for drinking water. Using water in this way can reduce the pressure we place on our freshwater systems. The reality of our water needs mean that in the future wastewater will be seen as a resource, not a waste product. Recycling and reusing treated waste water will save on the costs of providing clean water for household and cleaning use, as well as the costs to industry of clean water for cooling and processes.

Desalinisation plants can give access to freshwater in areas where there is very limited or no access to water.

In Abu Dhabi, oil is plentiful but water is scarce. Desalinisation plays a role in providing water to the Emirate.

Building management systems can allow us to understand how water is being used, captured and processed within a building. Before technologies are used to clean our water or turn sea water into drinking water, there are other measures that cities should take to reduce their water use. Significant amounts of clean water can be lost through leakages in our water systems. For example one quarter of London's water is lost through leakage between treatment plants and the tap. In 2010, Thames Water located and repaired 58,000 leaks in London's water infrastructure. Better monitoring, sensors and new infrastructure can all play their part in ensuring that less water is wasted in city systems. Tokyo has reduced its leakage rates from 20 percent to 3.6 percent. Implementing effective systems has saved $172 million in prevented expense by leakage control. Other cities must follow this example.

Cities can put in place monitors and sensors to ensure less water is lost through leaks.

Cities, their businesses and residents also need to be smarter about how much water they use. By monitoring water use through meters we can better understand how we use water and identify ways in which we can use less. In addition simple changes such as turning off the tap whilst brushing teeth, ensuring the washing machine is full when it is used or boiling just the amount of water we want to use in kettles can have an impact on how much we demand each day. These measures all sound simple but can put less pressure on our water systems.

In Tokyo, water leakage from pipes has been reduced from 20 percent to 3.6 percent.

Our rising demands for water will force us to rethink how we use water. It will mean that cities must approach water more holistically, integrating the water supply, waste water, river basin management, agricultural irrigation and the governance arrangements more effectively.

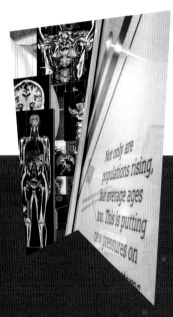

The Healthy Life zone is a reminder that a sustainable city is a healthy city.

Sustainability in healthcare is about focusing on prevention, rather than cure – encouraging healthy lifestyles and investing in better diagnosis to enable early treatment. The attractor for this zone was inspired by diagnostic imaging. A scan of a body is surrounded by close up diagnostic images of different bodyparts, using ultrasound, x-ray and MRI scans, among others. The attractor images are internally illuminated and the low voltage power to supply them is transmitted directly to the tensioned cables which support the image frames. This required some careful development with the same rigging company that installed the Go Electric light lines.

The design language reflects the team's thinking about the space as a kind of living, breathing entity in its own right, with the body as the key point of reference. The city grid is referenced in this zone with relation to the system of networks within our bodies: organic blood, veins, arteries, organs. The graphics are part of a cellular based structure, networked together to form large display walls.

The design is personal, rather than clinical, placing people at the heart of the story. Although displays remind us that life and health are fragile, content focuses on some of the astounding technologies that can lead to better lives.

There is a vertical connection to the Demographic Megatrend display on the mezzanine, reinforcing the direct link between health and demographics. A significant part of the zone is dedicated to a series of displays about healthy living. Some of the exhibits are presented as 'windows' offering views into our bodies, for example Catch it Early – using technology to identify and treat illness – and Personalised Medicine.

Other displays unpick details of the healthcare system, for example looking at ways of making healthcare more accessible, more mobile and more affordable.

A healthy city offers a physical and built environment that encourages, enables and supports health, recreation and well-being, safety, social interaction, accessibility and mobility, a sense of pride and cultural identity and is responsive to the needs of all its citizens.

The Zagreb Declaration for Healthy Cities.

Healthy Life

There is a pressing need for future cities to harvest enough water to supply an ever increasing urban population. In this chapter, we will look at the role of other urban infrastructures and technologies that shape physical, social and mental well being, focusing on urban form and diagnostic tools to sustain high levels of what we call 'chronic health'.

Underneath London's Embankment lies its main sewage network, built by the Victorians to improve the health of its citizens.

From urban pathologies to health advantages
Cities have come a long way since Dickens' and Engels' early records of a new type of megacentre harboring diseases such as tuberculosis and cholera. These urban pathologies preoccupied the revolutionary Victorian reformists, which ultimately led to the creation of the first planning authorities and city governments such as London's Metropolitan Board of Works.

Today, cities are continuing on these traditions and harnessing their economies of scale to concentrate high levels of health infrastructure from hospitals, to trained doctors, sanitation and clean water to deliver healthy environments. According to statistics by the World Health Organisation, infant mortality is lower in urban than in rural areas.

Inequalities within
However, challenges persist and urban health inequalities are striking in both developed and developing cities. The differences are very obvious when life expectancy is compared in cities such as London and Mumbai but they become even more striking when these inequalities exist within the city itself. In London for example, the life expectancy at birth of a citizen drops by seven years when one travels from the centre to the east on the Jubilee Line. In developing countries, the difference of basic health indicators between informal and formal areas is even more accentuated.

Accessibility
Access to basic health services underpins the performance of key health indicators but the challenge remains on how

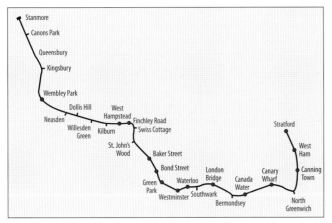

Life expectancy of Londoners decreases as you travel from the centre to the east on the Jubilee Line.

More and more cities are providing citizens with natural recreational ammenities within walking distance of their homes and places of work.

these services can be made truly universal. Too often health infrastructure investment is piecemeal with basic sanitation infrastructure covering only parts of the city. This leads to a splintering of the city fabric with high levels of health infrastructure only available to wealthier neighborhoods of the city that can pay for the benefits. Accessibility to health services may also be highly dependent on income as is the case of the US or based on rural and urban residency status as in the case of Chinese cities. It is believed that over 200 million Chinese urban dwellers do not have access to healthcare.

From prevention to chronic health

With nearly two-thirds of deaths globally now caused by non-infectious diseases such as lung and heart disease, it is

Las Vegas' sprawling low density discourages walking and increases the tendency of car use, which in turn shapes healthy lifestyles.

Amsterdam's dedicated cycle lanes encourage cycling whilst decreasing congestion and increasing physical well being.

important that health budgets are more and more geared towards prevention and towards what we call chronic health. Chronic health is a new concept showing how cities can nudge dwellers into healthy lifestyles over a long period of time such as encouraging more walking and more social interaction, which are important constituents of physical and mental well being.

At the same time, cities need to discourage car use and increase walking rates by providing public transportation.

Cities can start by designing typologies that include small urban blocks with high density streets and squares that encourage greater walkability as well protecting natural areas through green belts. In other words, health is as much the domain of architects and planners as that of doctors.

Hybrid buses in London provide a win-win situation. They decrease congestion whilst improving air quality.

Rapidly developing cities need to discourage the extensive use of the car, which congests roads and pollutes the urban environment.

Istanbul's metropolitan masterplan is trying to prevent growth in the northern part of the city which is an area of natural beauty and the main water source for the city.

Chronic health can also be improved with the latest monitoring technologies, which have direct health consequences as well as financial benefits in preventing more costly treatment programmes. Diagnostic imaging technologies are also important in personalizing medicine so that individual treatment plans are tailored to a patient's lifestyle.

A healthy city is a city for all its citizens: inclusive, supportive, sensitive and responsive to their diverse needs and expectations.

The Zagreb Declaration for Healthy Cities.

Brazil's Community Health Agents today and tomorrow
Over the last twenty years, a team of over 250,000 health agents have been providing community health care services in some of Brazil's most under-resourced areas. Once a month, a health agent visits one of her 150 designated households in her community to provide basic care and advice on a variety of specialties such as breastfeeding, screening uptake, chronic disease management and lifestyle. Equally important is the role of the Community Health Agent as a data gatherer on basic socio-economic assets on each household, which helps health authorities build a picture on the health and social profiles of thousands of neighborhoods across the country. The health agent therefore takes on many different roles including developing the social bond inherent in neighborhoods.

There is huge future potential for embedded agents to use connected diagnostic and data gathering devices such as pocket sized ultrasound scanners to scale the capacity of their operations. The symbiosis between technology and face to face interaction in local areas is an efficient way of providing affordable universal health care without the need to invest in secondary, capital intensive health centres.

Contemporary cities understand the importance of providing a universal and accessible health infrastructure concentrating on prevention through healthier lifestyles and routine diagnosis. Financing this infrastructure remains a big challenge but cities can start delivering such improvements, by providing an urban fabric that promotes walkability, a green fabric for leisure and outdoor activity and policies for lower emissions that lead to cleaner air. This is the focus of the next chapter.

We wanted people to feel like they were stepping out of the exhibition and into a natural environment. The green wall is a real, living entity, which feeds itself through an intelligent hydroponic system. The plants are all local species and the rocks in the cages at the base of the wall are hewn from a quarry in Essex. It doesn't require much water to live, but the water it does use is harvested from the rain.

Dan Savage, Exhibition Designer, Event Communications.

The Clean and Green zone borders Healthy Life and, like that zone, is inspired by nature. At the heart of Clean and Green is the living, green wall that forms a dramatic backdrop for displays examining the ways in which we can reduce, recycle, reuse. The plants are a reminder that the best-designed buildings resemble trees: sustainable and self-sufficient.

Orbs of 'air' rise up from the introduction panel, representing the different pollutants being produced by cities – with a mass of CO_2 sitting at the top, representing the rise of greenhouse gases.

Set into the green wall is information about different elements of the city environment: wildlife, pollution, biodiversity, habitats, emissions.

Graphic displays explain that cities both contribute to and suffer from the effects of air, water, light and noise pollution. What Are We Breathing is a software interactive that breaks down what's in the air that we breathe every day. Meeting the CO_2 Challenge is a software interactive that presents some of the issues and possible solutions for reducing our CO_2 output.

The quality of waste management services is a good indicator of a city's governance. The way in which waste is produced and discarded gives us a key insight into how people live.

Anna Tibaijuka, Under-Secretary General, United Nations, UN-Habitat.

Clean & Green

Successful and vibrant cities are places where people want to live and work and businesses want to locate and invest. Creating cities that are clean and green forms an important aspect of making cities attractive places to live and work.

Green spaces can help make cities more resilient to climate change and extreme weather.

Parks and open spaces: A city's green lungs

A city's natural green infrastructure – its parks and open spaces does not just provide areas for leisure, exercise and relaxation. Green spaces in cities can contribute towards a healthy mind as well and increase the value of land and property. They can also help make cities more resilient to climate change and extreme weather, cooling the city during hot weather, absorbing noise pollution and absorbing flood water. Green spaces act as the city's green lungs, absorbing and storing carbon, as well as providing habitats and ecosystems. More and more cities are adopting policies to increase tree cover or convert old pieces of city infrastructure into greenways. New York has

a target to plant one million trees over the next decade. It has also converted a historic rail freight line above the streets of Manhattan into a public park, the High Line.

New York has a target to plant one million trees over the next decade.

Vegetated roofs and walls, roof terraces and roof gardens also play an important role in greening cities. They can help reduce the amount and speed of storm water run-off reaching water systems, as well as keeping buildings cooler in hot spells. London has trialed living green walls to see the impact they can have in trapping air pollutants. Planting vegetation in busy streets in cities can reduce street-level concentrations by as much as 40 percent for NO_2 and 60 percent for particulate matter (PM). Other approaches in pollution hotspots have included the use of dust suppressants to reduce

PM_{10} along some roads and industrial sites, which has reduced concentrations by 16 percent and up to 59 percent respectively.

Brussels

European cities have challenging targets to improve their air quality set by the European Union.

Tackling air pollution

Air pollution is a challenge for all cities. Our homes, transport and workplaces all contribute to air pollution. It has been a challenge for cities for centuries. Police in Tokyo were regulating boilers in the city as early as 1877. In 1661 John Evelyn presented King Charles II with a treatise arguing that smoke pollution would shorten the lives of people living in London. Various laws in the 19th century were enforced by the Police to control smoke and nuisance. However, it was not until the London fog of 1952 that serious action was taken to limit smoke emissions. The 1952 episode was estimated to lead to between 3,500 to 4,000 more deaths than would have been expected under normal conditions.

Air pollution is a challenge for many global cities.

The types of pollution and their sources can vary from city to city. Two of the most challenging pollutants are particulate matter (PM) and nitrogen oxides (NOx). The World Health Organisation (WHO) estimates that more than two million people die every year from breathing tiny particulates present in air pollution. Sources of air pollution include transportation and the burning of fossil fuels in power stations, factories, offices and homes as well as from the incineration of waste. It also comes from natural sources such as organic compounds from vegetation, ground dust and salt spray from seas and oceans.

Public transportation, cleaner vehicles, eco-driving and ensuring traffic flows are all important to reducing air pollution.

Whilst there is no-one simple solution there are technologies that can help reduce air pollution in cities. Over 70 European cities have introduced or are introducing a low emission zone, where the most polluting vehicles are banned from all or parts of cities. Berlin, Cologne and Hannover were the earliest adopters in January 2008.

Cities need to put in place effective systems to collect waste for recycling.

Effective public transportation infrastructure, cleaner vehicles, eco-driving and ensuring the smooth flow of traffic play an important role in reducing the sources of air pollution in cities. Battery electric vehicles and hydrogen fuel cell vehicles both have zero tail pipe emissions – providing obvious benefits in city environments. However, to be truly green, we will need to move away from producing electricity from burning fossil fuels and produce hydrogen fuel from renewable sources such as from waste derived biogas.

Seoul hopes to meet 20 percent of its energy demand from renewable energy by 2020, half of which will come from hydrogen fuel cells.

Wasting a resource

Waste is another challenge for cities. In the worst instances, cities have no or few services in place to manage it. It is allowed to pollute land and water in unregulated sites and is a hazard to health. However, when managed well, waste is a valuable resource which can be used to generate green energy for our cities or to make new products. Cities need to approach the management of waste using the waste hierarchy. Reducing waste in the first place and reusing waste items where possible. Where this is not possible it should be recycled or have the energy recovered. Waste can be used to generate electricity, whilst the heat produced from that process can be captured and used to heat or cool buildings. The last and least desirable option for most types of waste is the disposal of waste to landfill.

Sustainable cities have systems in place to collect waste for recycling. These materials are then turned into new products. However, to close the loop, cities and their citizens need to ensure that they are purchasing recycled goods or products containing recycled materials. Waste that cannot be recycled can often be used to generate power and provide heating through district networks to homes in cities. Over 40 million tonnes of waste are thermally treated in Japan. As well as incineration, alternative waste to energy technologies are developing and playing an important role globally. These include pyrolysis, gasification and anaerobic digestion.

Cities need to view waste as a resource not a problem.

Feeding cities

With an increasing global population, there are more mouths to feed. Agriculture places a significant toll on resources such as water. It can cause pollution, is energy intensive and lead to loss of habitat. There are a number of solutions such as organic agriculture and better pest control. In cities more and more citizens are looking at urban farming, offering food as locally as possible. This decreases food miles associated with transporting food to cities, whilst offering benefits such as fresher and seasonal produce. Urban farming can also make our cities greener and reduce run-off in cities and reduce the impact of the urban heat island in cities. Whilst urban farming is currently at a small scale, cities of the future may well have vertical farms producing much of the food we consume. It may well seem a long way off but the community's benefits and reduction in the impact of food may drive this forward. It is not uncommon now for produce such as honey to be produced on rooftops in city neighborhoods, who is to say how much more produce may be grown and produced vertically in our cities of the future?

Cologne is among over 70 European cities that have or are planning low emission zones.

Zero energy buildings

flood monitoring for emerg
forecast and management

When you look round I think you're going to find that this ambition is so contagious that you're going to leave here with a feeling that you've seen the future and the future is good.

Eric Pickles, Secretary of State for Communities and Local
Government, UK.

After exploring the Megatrends on the Mezzanine and the Macro zones on the ground floor, you are invited to experience the world of 2050 in Future Life. Will the future be as dark, dreary and dysfunctional as it's usually painted in sci-fi movies? Or will it the future simply be a smarter, more sustainable version of the present?

The Future Life space, sitting at the core of the Crystal, is a culmination of the whole experience. Based on a Siemens research project called Pictures of the Future, this zone was developed as the final destination for the exhibition, where all the solutions you have learnt about in the Macro zones can be shown being put into practice in an imagined future.

Consoles enable you to 'check in' with your Crystal Key tag, seeing how many crystals you've gathered throughout your visit and touching on them to find out more about introducing sustainable practices into your daily life.

The atmosphere of the space is relaxed and intimate, inviting you to enjoy the floor-to-ceiling presentation of Future Life.

What might life in a city look like in 2050? Well, for example, instead of owning equipment or property (cars, workspaces, gardens) people might borrow or rent them for just as long as they need them. There may be more high rise buildings, but they might have gardens and even beehives built on their roofs. Cities might be bigger, but they will have more – not fewer – green spaces.

The future here might be imaginary, but there was a desire to avoid the clichéd visions of the future. The three cities of New York, London and Copenhagen are shown as example future cities and the starting point for the film was what these cities look like now. Many of the buildings and structures that exist today will still be there in 50, 100, 200 years.

Image: © Event Communications Ltd

Image: © Event Communications Ltd / Franck Follet Photography

This city now doth, like a garment, wear the beauty of the morning; silent bare, ships, towers, domes, theatres and temples lie open unto the fields and to the sky; All bright and glittering in the smokeless air.

William Wordsworth (1770-1850) English Romantic poet.

Future Life

So what might our future cities look like? In the future, high-rise buildings will be like small towns, with homes, shops, workshops – even gardens and farms – all under one roof. The spaces around will be flexible, changing to match our needs. Instead of owning things, we will pay to use a space or an item, then give it back, hand it off, or recycle after use. For example, we will invite friends to ride along in shared e-cars and rent space in community gardens. We may even order produce from our community gardens.

Technology and fluidity will enable us to live efficient lives. Many people will work from home, switching between business and leisure, the real and the virtual. Our new lifestyle will allow neighbours to join together in vibrant, dynamic communities. Buildings today account for the bulk of a city's energy consumption and greenhouse gas emissions. They represent enormous potential for energy savings and are key to sustainable city development.

In the future, buildings will be self-sufficient, producing a surplus of energy, recycling their own waste, minimising water usage, collecting rainwater, and reusing and recycling grey water. Buildings will also be fully automated and intelligent, with thousands of sensors making sure that lights are switched on or off, and that rooms are optimally heated only when they are occupied.

Shanghai is preparing for the future with transport networks designed for the modern metropolis.

Tokyo, the world's largest city, is thinking big. A Sky City building is being planned, two times taller than the tallest existing building in the world to accommodate the expanding population of Tokyo. A city of the future, in the sky.

The lifeblood of urban existence – renewable energy – will flow along main arteries to power the city. The smart grid will respond, communicating with all producers and consumers. But residents will not just consume electricity; they will generate and store it. They can use surplus energy to do things like charge their electric cars. Their city will make energy miners and energy traders of us all.

Sensors throughout the city will provide essential information to keep it running efficiently and to keep people safe. The city will become a living organism, seeing, hearing and thinking. It will be intelligent and responsive. Real-time information will flow into the city control center, where it will be integrated and visualized. Traffic lights and information systems will be adapted so traffic flows smoothly. Data will also be used for urban planning. Residents will be invited to take an active part in the planning process and help decide the future of their communities. Residents will have a direct connection to public services and can participate at every level. This will be a city that responds to the needs of its population.

Journeys across the city will take people and packages from one mode of transport to another via mega hubs. When you set out to meet friends, a navigation assistant will plan your route. It will begin by a booked e-car to the local transport hub. Payment will be invisible; the public transportation network will recognise you and ensures a seamless journey. If there's a traffic accident or road construction, the navigation assistant will instantly respond by changing your route.

By managing our urban transport, cities can ensure that people keep moving as congestion becomes a thing of the past.

While most people sleep, the city will restock, recharge and recycle. Public transport will be used to deliver goods and packages. When energy demand is low, the smart grid will recharge the city's batteries and tasks that can be done overnight will be automatically activated. Our future city never sleeps – its cycle continues.

In the future, cities will change dramatically to meet the needs of their residents and respond to the emerging trends of an increasing global population. Providing the necessary services to cater for the changing demographic, and to provide the critical infrastructure that is needed to live and work in an evolving world means that cities will become more dynamic and more agile in the way they operate and how they tackle these ever present challenges.

London in the future.

Today, we live in a digital world, providing the opportunity to better understand how we live and how that lifestyle impacts the world around us. In the future, this information will be used to help cities plan and deliver the services that its citizens require.

Tel Aviv, one of the most innovative cities in the world has adapted its urban landscape to accommodate the digital economy.

The desire to travel and to be connected to people and places means our cities need to keep moving, but they will do so faster, and with less impact on the environment. Cities will also ensure that people can live and work in a safe environment, providing them with security and confidence against the perceived threats of modern day urban life.

New York City adapting to the needs of the future, surrounded by its historic and cultural heritage.

New York City in the future.

Individuals will play a part in the future city through their interactions with the buildings in which they live and work. Reducing impacts on natural resources is inextricably linked to how we design, build and behave in our buildings, and through the use of smart technology in buildings we will preserve the world's most precious resources. Managing our energy use at a city scale by electrifying our networks will allow us to further conserve these resources. Understanding where energy is being used and when, will eliminate wasteful consumption.

Globally, water scarcity will also begin to change how water is used and the importance we will place on conservation. Optimizing our water distribution networks will ensure that everyone is provided with the clean drinking water that is so critical to leading a healthy life. Quality of life will also be enhanced by the changes that technology will make to reduce pollution in our environment through the air that we breathe and the water we drink.

Creating the future city means placing the environment at the forefront of future growth. It means enabling change with innovation in place making, foresight in decision making and harnessing technological advancements to deliver the critical requirements of daily life that have become fundamental to our basic needs.

The battle for tackling climate change will be won or lost in our cities. Through human history cities have overcome many challenges and evolved through their innovation. The path to a sustainable future requires strong leadership, innovative technology and a step change in the pace of deployment that only cities can make happen.

Martin Powell, Head of Urban Development, Siemens Centre of Competence Cities (Former Environment Advisor to the Mayor of London and Former Special Advisor to C40 Cities).

The role of future cities is to combine the old with the new, whilst protecting and optimising quality of life.

Copenhagen in the future.

THE Crystal

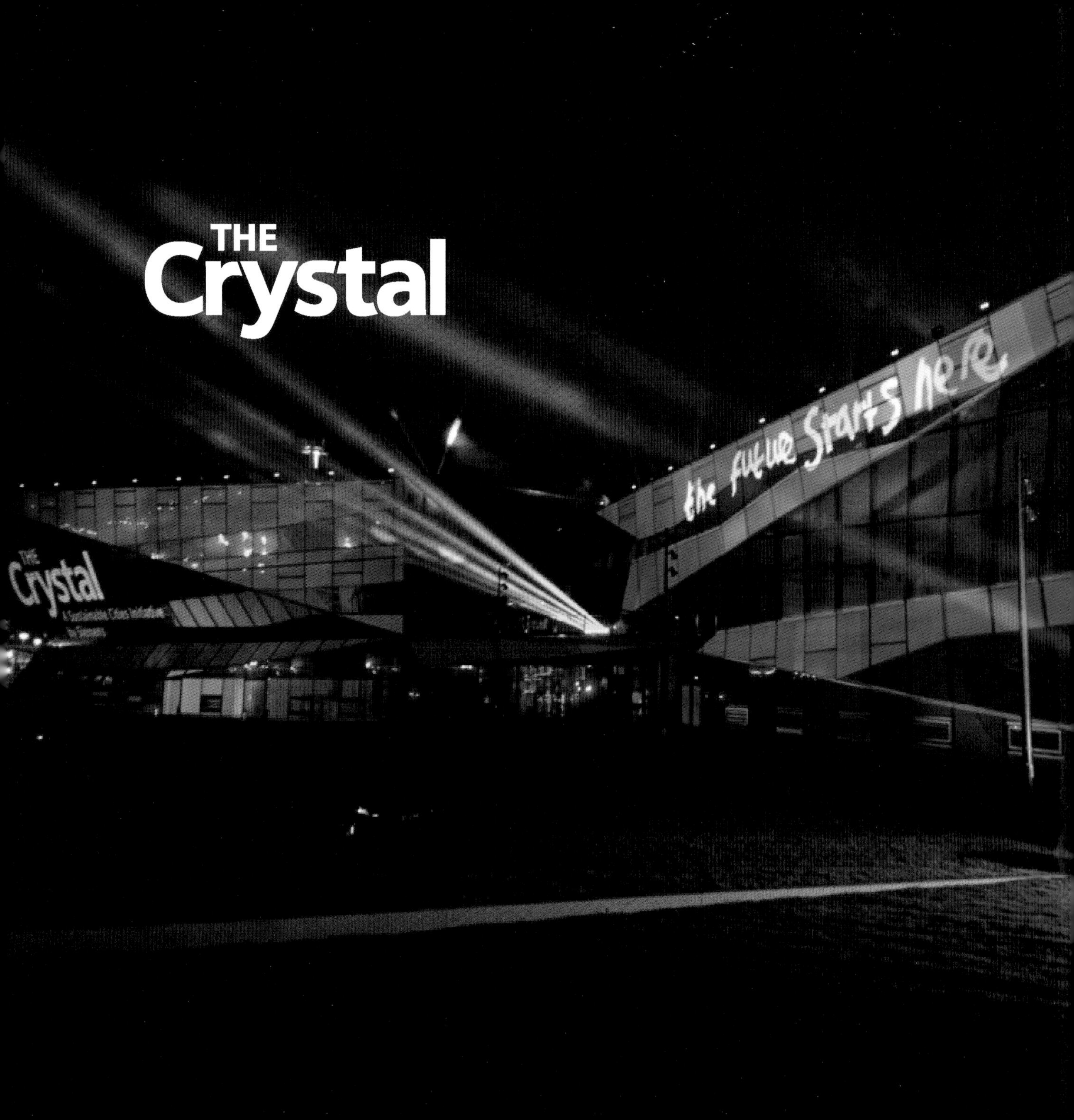

The Crystal

The Crystal, one of London's newest landmark buildings, has been designed to set a new standard for high performance green buildings. It walks the talk - actively educating and inspiring all of us about urban sustainability and the future role of technology in our lives.

The building houses the largest exhibition on urban sustainability in the world, highlights the challenges facing our cities across the globe and showcases how technology and innovation is meeting those challenges. The exhibition is interactive and has elements of interest for those new to urban sustainability and for professionals in the field. The building offers an auditorium and conference suite to create a hub and build a dialogue among the professionals working in the field of urban sustainability.

The building's crystalline shape symbolizes the different facets of sustainability and the range of advanced building technologies available. It is the first building in the world to simultaneously achieve the globally recognised standard of LEED Platinum as well as the UK's BREEAM Outstanding. The buildings innovative design means its consumption of electricity is 50 percent lower than comparable buildings and its carbon footprint is 60 percent lower than international benchmarks.

The building design is based around reductive and responsive principles. The Crystal is designed to need as little energy as possible, supply the energy using low carbon sources and to apply state of the art control to ensure that it constantly seeks to minimise it's use of energy in real time.

The Crystal's performance starts with a building envelope that is tuned to the local climate. The angular geometry and careful use of glass combine to give a building that is 75 percent day lit and where the geometry is designed to keep unwanted summer sun out and allow winter sun in. The envelope is highly insulated against the cold winters and windy river conditions. When the climate is milder the building can be naturally ventilated using computer controlled opening windows.

To meet the residual energy demand of the building the systems include a series of low energy systems. As well as using exceptionally efficient heat recovery the building is heated entirely using ground source heating. The building's excess summer heat is stored in the soil under the building using a network of 17km of buried pipework. This same energy is then drawn back out in the winter and used to heat the building.

The roof of the building includes two arrays to gain solar energy. The first is for solar hot water heating and meets 60 percent of the buildings demand for hot water. And the second is of photovoltaic modules generating 17.5 percent of the buildings electricity using the sun. The balance of the buildings energy use is all electricity. No gas or other fossil fuel is burned in the building. Being 'all-electric' is an essential element of the building's response to the future of our urban areas. As the power grid becomes cleaner (as we use more low carbon energy) and we reduce our reliance on fossil fuels, more buildings will tend towards using only electricity. The Crystal makes that leap now and demonstrates that all electric buildings are possible today.

As part of the building's future agenda it is 'smart grid ready'. That means the building can regulate its energy use according to the availability of power in the electricity grid. This is an important feature for a future where our electricity supply will include power generated by the sun and wind, neither of which are constant. By having buildings like the Crystal that can vary their power use minute by minute we can match the power demand of our cities to the available supply without compromising the comfort or quality of life of the people who live in them. To achieve this the Crystal's control system uses over 3,354 data connections to talk to each component right down to every individual light. The control system can then reduce the electricity demand of each one in response to the available power starting with the components that have little or no effect on the comfort and experience of the people inside.

The Crystal applies a similar rigour to the use of water. The demand for water is reduced by using toilets, basins and showers which use as little water as possible. The residual demand is met by using treated rainwater, reusing water from basins and sinks and even by treating and cleaning flushed water from toilets.

The result is a building that uses 90 percent less water than equivalent buildings. In the winter, the building is so efficient that the water cycle closes completely and none of the water comes from the mains water supply.

The real day to day operation of the Crystal is as important as its design concepts - contrary to popular belief buildings never perform as the computer models suggest because they have the unpredictable variable of human behavior to factor in. The exhibition includes a display board showing publicly how much energy and water are being used and generated by the building. By tracking how the building actually operates, by guiding the people who use it to make sensible decisions and by acting as a test bed for new technologies as they emerge, the building will continue to be a living model for urban buildings.

The Crystal is a symbol of what is possible in design, construction and operation in the world today. It was built to show that a step change is possible to achieve the highest levels of building performance without compromise to the people who use it. The building's use of resources has been minimized and optimized to embody what is possible and indeed what is required in our cities today if they are to survive and compete in the future.

Bibliography

Barratt, Ben; Carslaw, Gary; Green, David; Tremper, A. (2012). Evaluation of the impact of dust suppressant application on ambient PM10 concentrations in London.

Davies, Zoe; Edmondson, Jill; Heinemeyer, Andreas; Leak, J. (2011). Mapping an urban ecosystem service: Quanitifying above ground carbon storage at a city-wide scale. Journal of Applied Ecology.

Field, C. (2012). Managing the risks of extreme events and disasters to advance climate change adaption: special report of the Intergovernmental Panel on Climate Change. New York: Cambridge University Press.

Hutchinson, David; Tonooka, Yutaka; Kannari, Akiyoshi; Nishida, Yuko; Vowles, D. (2010). Air Quality in London and Tokyo: A comparison.

International Energy Agency. (2012). Key World Energy Statistics 2012. Paris.

International Energy Agency. (2013a). A Tale of Renewed Cities. Paris.

International Energy Agency. (2013b). Redrawing the energy-climate map. Paris.

International Energy Agency; Organisation for Economic Co-operation and Development. (2012). World energy outlook, 2012. Paris.

Jacobs, J. (1961). The death and life of great American cities. New York: Random House.

Johnson, S. (2006). The ghost map: the story of London's most terrifying epidemic--and how it changed science, cities, and the modern world. New York: Riverhead Books.

Karlaftis, M.G; Latoski, S.P; Richards, N.J; Sinha, K. C. (1999). ITS Impacts on Safety and Traffic Management: An Investigation of Secondary Crashes. ITS Journal, 7(1), 39-52.

LSE Cities. (2011). Cities Health and Wellbeing. In Report on a conference organised by LSE Cities and the Alfred Herrhausen Society in partnership with the University of Hong Kong. London.

McKinsey Global Institute. (2012). Urban world: cities and the rise of the consuming class.

Pearce, David; Moran, D. (1994). The Economic Value of Biodiversity.

Perez, C. (2002). Technological revolutions and financial capital: the dynamics of bubbles and golden ages. Northampton: Cheltenham.

Pugh, Thomas; MacKenzie, Robert; Whyatt, Duncan; Hewitt, N. (2012). Effectiveness of green infrastructure for improvement of air quality in urban street canyons. Lancaster.

Smith, Joel; Schneider, S. (2009). Assessing dangerous climate change through an update of the Intergovernmental Panel on Climate Change (IPCC) "reasons for concern." Proceedings of the National Academy of Sciences.

Stern, N. H. (2007). The economics of climate change: the Stern review. Cambridge University Press.

Stiglitz, Joseph; Sen, Amartya; Fitoussi, J. P. (2010). Mismeasuring our lives: why GDP doesn't add up: the report. New York: New Press;Distributed by Perseus Distribution.

Suzuki, Hiroaki; Cervero, Robert; Iuchi, K. (2013). Transforming cities with transit: transit and land-use integration for sustainable urban development. Washington, D.C.: World Bank.

UN-Habitat. (2010). Solid waste management in the world's cities: water and sanitation in the world's cities 2010. Washington, D.C.

United Nations Department of Economic and Social Affairs. (2011). World Urbanisation Prospects. The 2011 Revision.

United Nations Department of Economic and Social Affairs; World Meteorological Organisation. (1992). International Conference on Water and the Environment: keynote papers.

United Nations. Department of Economic and Social Affairs. Population Division. (2011). World Population Prospects: the 2010 revision. New York.

Welsh, B; Farrington, D. (2009). Public Area CCTV and Crime Prevention: An Updated Systematic Review and Meta-Analysis. Justice Quarterly, 26(4), 716-745.

Wolf, Aaron; Wolfe, Shira; Giordano, M. (2003). International waters: indicators for identifying basins at risk. Paris.

World Health Organisation. (2009). Zagreb Declaration for Healthy Cities.

World Health Organisation. (2012). Addressing the social determinants of health: the urban dimension and the role of local government. Copenhagen.

World Health Organisation; UNICEF. (2005). Water for life: making it happen. Geneva.

World Wildlife Fund. (2011). Big Cities. Big Water. Big Challenges. Water in an urbanising world. Berlin.

Published by Booklink
Publisher: Dr Claude Costecalde
www.booklink.ie
© Photographs and text, The Crystal, 2013
© Design, Booklink, 2013
ISBN: 978-1-906886-57-8
Printed in Slovenia

EDITED BY

Pedro Pires de Miranda & Martin Powell

Authors

Julie Alexander, Pete Daw, Stefan Denig, Eithne Owens, Dave Richards, Elaine Trimble, Savvas Verdis and the Event Communications team.

Acknowledgements

Carsten Becker, Thomas Brodocz, Alex Clement-Jones, Klaus Heidinger, Joachim Kiauk, Werner Kruckow , Christine Kuhn, Juergen Loos, Josh Palmer, Pablo Vaggione, Willfried Wienholt and the Centre of Competence Cities team at the Crystal.

Special Thanks

Roland Aurich, Michael R Bloomberg, Roland Busch, Joan Clos, Frank Jensen, Boris Johnson, Daniel Libeskind - for their Thought Leadership and contributions to the exhibition.

Exhibition chapters: © Event Communications Ltd / Franck Follet Photography
Other images: Shutterstock